Understanding Patriarchal Blessings

Shea,   Jan. 4, 03
      Happy 15th birthday!
We love you.
We hope you'll enjoy
this book.
      Love,
        Dad & Mom

Understanding Patriarchal Blessings

R. Clayton Brough • Thomas W. Grassley

Eighth Printing: February 2002

International Standard Book Number:
0-88290-253-9

Horizon Publishers' Catalog and Order Number:
1049

Printed and distributed
in the United States of America by

**Horizon
Publishers**
& Distributors, Incorporated

Mailing Address:
P.O. Box 490
Bountiful, Utah 84011-0490

Street Address:
50 South 500 West
Bountiful, Utah 84010

Local Phone: (801) 295-9451
Toll Free: 1 (866) 818-6277
FAX: (801) 295-0196

E-mail: horizonp@burgoyne.com
Internet: http://www.horizonpublishers.biz

Dedicated to all Patriarchs.

Acknowledgment

The authors wish to thank officials of The Church of Jesus Christ of Latter-day Saints and the Church Historical Department who helped in providing appropriate information and insight into the subject of patriarchal blessings.

Also, the authors sincerely appreciate the editorial help of B. William Silcock, Cathy Lynn Silcock and David R. James; and, most importantly, the encouragement and sustaining love of our wives and children.

Preface

This book has been written to answer questions about patriarchal blessings. Most of the material and statements in this publication come from remarks by Presidents of The Church of Jesus Christ of Latter-day Saints, Patriarchs to the Church, and other General Authorities. Additional information comes from selected Church publications and LDS authors.

The reader should be aware that this is not an official Church publication and that the authors of this book are solely responsible for the manner in which documented material is presented. It is appropriate that those who read this book seek inspiration from the Holy Ghost in understanding the information contained herein.

Preparing this book has been an enjoyable experience.

We hope that those who read it will find the contents informative and rewarding.

Contents

Dedication 5

Acknowledgment 6

Preface 7

1. The Office of a Patriarch 11
   The History of Patriarchs 11
   The Purpose for Having Church Patriarchs 16
   How Patriarchs are Chosen 17
   The Priesthood of a Patriarch 18
   The Office of "Patriarch to the Church" 18
   The Position and Responsibility of Stake Patriarchs 20
   The Preparation of Patriarchs 21
   The Two Types of Patriarchs: Ordained and Natural 24

2. The Definition of a Patriarchal Blessing . . 31
   Defining "Patriarchal Blessings" 31
   The Difference Between Patriarchal Blessings
      and Other Blessings 32
   The Difference Between Patriarchal Blessings
      and Fortunetelling 37

3. The Purpose of a Patriarchal Blessing . . . 43
   The Declaration of Lineage 43
   Understanding Who We Are
      and What We Can Achieve 46
   An Instrument for Encouragement and Comfort . . 48

4. The Contents of a Patriarchal Blessing . . . 53
   What Patriarchal Blessings Usually Contain 53
   The Heading of Patriarchal Blessings 53
   The Opening of Patriarchal Blessings 54
   The Body or General Text of Patriarchal Blessings . 55
   The Closing of Patriarchal Blessings 57
   Scriptural Examples of Patriarchal Blessings . . . 58

5. Preparing for a Patriarchal Blessing 61
Patriarchal Blessings Are for All Church Members . 61
When to Receive a Patriarchal Blessing 63
Missionaries & Patriarchal Blessings 65
The Steps in Obtaining a Patriarchal Blessing 67

6. Receiving a Patriarchal Blessing 73
A Patriarch's Interview and Blessing 73
Receiving Written Copies of Patriarchal Blessings . 75
One Patriarchal Blessing Is Usually Enough 77

7. Understanding a Patriarchal Blessing 81
How to Understand or Interpret
    Patriarchal Blessings 81
People Can Be from Different Lineages
    —Even Within Families 82
Patriarchal Blessings Do Not Outline
    Everything That Will Happen 85
Promises Within a Patriarchal Blessing
    Are Conditioned Upon Faithful Living 87
Patriarchal Blessings Should Be Viewed
    from an Eternal Perspective 89
People Should Use Discretion When Sharing
    or Discussing Patriarchal Blessings 95
Patriarchal Blessings Should Be Read
    Periodically and Prayerfully 96

8. Living a Patriarchal Blessing 99
Acquire Appreciation for the
    Significance of Patriarchal Blessings 99
Faithfulness Brings Fulfillment
of Patriarchal Blessings 101

Bibliography 103
Index 107
About the Authors 111

1

The Office of a Patriarch

The History of Patriarchs

Anciently, the span of time from Adam to Moses was known as the "Patriarchal Age." During this period great leaders such as Adam, Abraham and other "patriarchs" pronounced upon their posterity magnificent "blessings" such as those given by Jacob to his twelve sons, which "predicted what would happen to them and their posterity after them" (Genesis 49).[1] These blessings were "Patriarchal blessings" and they were given in each generation by the oldest worthy male member of each family. Literally translated, "patriarch" (which is pronounced "pa-tri-ar-chal," not "pa-tri-art-i-cal") means "chief father," since "patri" or "padre" means "father," and "arch" means "chief." Therefore, the words "patriarch" and "father" are rather synonymous.[2]

During the Patriarchal Age, the patriarchal office was hereditary in nature. When Adam passed away, his son Seth became patriarch to

Adam's posterity. When Seth died, his son Enos became patriarch. This procedure was carried on throughout the Patriarchal Age with the eldest worthy son becoming patriarch in his father's place. (See D&C 107:40-52.)

In Christ's time, the organized Church still included the office of patriarch or "evangelist," "for the perfecting of the saints (Ephesians 4:12). However, the word "patriarch" itself only appears three times in the New Testament (Acts 2:29, 7:8, and Hebrews 7:4), and all three of these scriptures refer to patriarchs in the Old Testament. Nevertheless, the Prophet Joseph Smith explained that patriarchs or evangelists are one and the same:

> An evangelist is a patriarch, even the oldest man of the blood of Joseph or of the seed of Abraham. Wherever the Church of Christ is established on the earth, there should be a patriarch for the benefit of the posterity of the Saints, as it was with Jacob in giving his patriarchal blessings unto his sons.[3]

In our dispensation of time the office of patriarch has played an important role in the organization of the Church. Elder LeGrand Richards has explained:

> . . . The calling of a patriarch . . . is a very, very important calling—so important that in the organization of the Church, in the 107 Section of the Doctrine and Covenants, there is a command from the Lord that the Quorum of the Twelve in all the larger branches of the Church should call

patriarchs, or "evangelical ministers" as they are called in the revelation. The Prophet Joseph [Smith] explained that that was the calling of a patriarch, and that they were to ordain them and set them apart to bless the great family of the church. Now in ancient days the patriarchs blessed their own families, but since every man cannot be a patriarch in his own home the Lord has made provision that patriarchs should be called in all the larger branches of the Church.[4]

The first "ordained" patriarch in this last dispensation was Joseph Smith Sr. On December 18, 1833, Joseph Smith, Oliver Cowdery, Sidney Rigdon and Fredrick G. Williams ordained Joseph Smith Sr. to the office of Patriarch to the Church.[5] Joseph Smith Sr. did not preside over the Church itself, but served as Patriarch to the Church giving patriarchal blessings to those worthy to receive them. However, prior to this:

The first patriarchal blessings given in this dispensation were given by the Prophet Joseph Smith himself. He had every right to give patriarchal blessings because, not only was he a high priest and apostle, but a patriarch, in fact, holding all the keys and all the rights and the privileges of the priesthood. Oliver Cowdery, in recording some of the blessings that the Prophet gave called attention to the fact that he was the first patriarch of the Church—not ordained to give patriarchal blessings, but with the authority and power to give those blessings if he needed to and wished to because he held all the keys of the priesthood. He gave blessings; the first to be given to his father and his mother, to Oliver Cowdery, Hyrum, Samuel and William Smith, his brothers. He later gave other blessings.[6]

Joseph Smith Sr. was the first ordained patriarch to be sustained as a "prophet, seer and revelator," just as every Patriarch to the Church has been sustained since. And just as it was anciently, the office of Patriarch to the Church in this dispensation has generally followed the proper hereditary lines down to Eldred G. Smith—the current Patriarch Emeritus to the Church—in the following manner:

> From Joseph Smith Sr., to his eldest living son Hyrum, who was called out of the First Presidency of the Church to be ordained to this important position. (D&C 124:91-93). Alvin Smith was Joseph Smith Sr.'s oldest son and probably would have been the Patriarch to the Church if he had not passed away November 19, 1823, leaving Hyrum the oldest.
>
> When Hyrum was martyred, his oldest son John was only eleven years old and thus too young to preside, so Hyrum's younger brother William was called to succeed him. William was ordained Patriarch to the Church on May 24, 1845 by the Quorum of the Twelve, but was rejected by the Church membership at the conference held on October 6,1845. As a result of this, William is not considered an official Patriarch to the Church. Commenting on this matter, President Joseph F. Smith has said: "Because of [the lack of a sustaining vote at conference], William Smith should not be classed among the patriarchs

holding this exalted position, and for that reason, in speaking of the Presiding Patriarchs, William Smith has not been included."

Asael Smith, a brother to Joseph Smith Sr., was never set apart nor sustained as Presiding Patriarch either, but served for three years until his death on July 20, 1848. The first official Patriarch to the Church after Hyrum Smith was John Smith, Joseph Smith Sr.'s youngest brother, ordained by Brigham Young and Heber C. Kimball in 1849. John served until 1854, when another John Smith—Hyrum's son and the original successor to the position—was ordained in February 1855. By then, John was twenty-three years old and considered mature enough to fill the calling he was previously too young for. John, who was also ordained by Brigham Young, served fifty-six years, giving over 21,000 blessings to worthy recipients. John was then succeeded by his grandson Hyrum G. Smith, who in 1912 was ordained by Joseph F. Smith and served for nineteen years, giving 21,590 blessings until his death in 1932. After Hyrum G. Smith's death, Nicholas G. Smith was called and ordained a stake patriarch to serve the Salt Lake Stake. He was also authorized to give blessings to missionaries and those living where no ordained patriarch lived, but he was not considered the Presiding Patriarch.[7]

The successor to Nicholas Smith was George F. Richards—the first person not of the Smith family to serve even temporarily in the office of Patriarch to the Church, and he was called by President Heber J. Grant and sustained at General Conference in October 1937 as Acting Patriarch to the

Church. Elder Richards was a patriarch in the Tooele Utah Stake at the time of his calling.

He was followed by Joseph F. Smith who served for four years (from 1942 to 1946) and then was released to ill health

Eldred G. Smith—the current Patriarch Emeritus to the Church—is the great-great-grandson of Hyrum Smith, and was ordained on April 10, 1947. On October 6, 1979, Elder Eldred Smith was named to "emeritus status."[8]

The Purpose for Having Church Patriarchs

Within The Church of Jesus Christ of Latter-day Saints, the primary purpose and function of ordained patriarchs is to give "patriarchal blessings." It is through receiving such a blessing that a recipient can have his or her "lineage" declared, and when the patriarch is "so moved upon by the Spirit" also receive "an inspired and prophetic statement" of his or her life's mission.[9]

President John Taylor has said: "A Patriarch to the Church is appointed to bless those who are orphans or have no father in the church to bless them . . . where the church is so extensive . . . other patriarchs [such as stake patriarchs] have been ordained . . . to assist the Patriarch to the Church."[10] Furthermore, Elder John A. Widtsoe has stated: "There are many members of the church whose fathers or nearest male relatives are not in the church, or unfitted or unwilling to bless their children. For them special provision must be made."[11] That provision has been made through calling and ordaining the Patriarch to the Church and the many stake patriarchs throughout the world.

How Patriarchs are Chosen

The Doctrine and Covenants proclaims: "It is the duty of the Twelve [Apostles] in all large branches of the church to ordain evangelical ministers [or patriarchs], as they shall be designated unto them by revelation" (D&C 107:39). So patriarchs are selected by revelation and ordained by members of the Council of the Twelve.[12] Their authority is derived from the President of the Church in whom the ultimate power of giving such blessings on earth is vested.[13] A Church publication further states:

> Stake patriarchs are chosen by members of the Council of the Twelve. Although the stake president does not nominate the patriarch, he may suggest to a member of the Council of the Twelve the need for a patriarch. He may be asked for suggestions to be considered. The member of the Council of the Twelve, guided by the Spirit, will know who is to be the new patriarch or patriarchs for the stake.
>
> When a patriarch is selected, unless otherwise directed by a member of the Council of the Twelve, he will be sustained in a stake conference, and ordained by [his stake president or] a member of the Twelve or the First Presidency. He will [then] be instructed in his duties. . . .[14]

The Priesthood of a Patriarch

Patriarchs, whether it be the Patriarch to the Church or stake patriarchs, are high priests of the Melchizedek Priesthood. Furthermore:

> One of the offices in the Melchizedek Priesthood is that of patriarch. Those so chosen and ordained are called to give patriarchal blessings to worthy members of the Church. Ordained patriarchs include the Patriarch to the Church and stake patriarchs, with one or more in each stake.[15]

The Office of "Patriarch to the Church"

The person who serves as Patriarch to the Church is considered one of the General Authorities of the Church and "stands next in order to the members of the Council of the Twelve Apostles."[16] Of the man who holds this office the Lord has said: "He shall hold the keys of the patriarchal blessings upon the heads of all my people" (D&C 124:92). In addition, a Church publication states:

> The Patriarch to the Church, when requested, gives patriarchal blessings to Church members who have been properly recommended in their stakes or missions where no local patriarch is available. He does not preside over or supervise the stake patriarchs.[17]

Further insight into the office of Patriarch to the Church is provided by the following commentary:

. . . [On January 19, 1841] a revelation was given to Joseph Smith elevating the office of Patriarch in the organization of the Church:

"Verily, thus saith the Lord unto you, my servant Joseph Smith. . . . And from this time forth I appoint unto him [Hyrum Smith] that he may be a prophet, and a seer, and a revelator unto my church, as well as my servant Joseph." (D&C 124:1,94.)

This title of being a "prophet, seer and revelator" is only given to the First Presidency, the Council of the Twelve Apostles and to the Patriarch to the Church. . . . However . . . the Patriarch has not had a major role in the leadership of the Church and . . . in the event that all of the members of the First Presidency and the Council of the Twelve Apostles were to die simultaneously, the role of Church leadership would fall to the First Council of Seventy and not to the Patriarch [of the Church]. This is in accord with a "revelation on Priesthood, given through Joseph Smith . . . at Kirtland, Ohio, dated March 28, 1835." (D&C107, Preface.) In it he wrote:

"Three presiding High Priests . . . form a quorum of the Presidency of the church. . . . The Twelve Apostles . . . form a quorum, equal in authority and power to the three presidents previously mentioned. The seventy are also called to preach the gospel . . . And they form a quorum equal in authority to that of the Twelve special witnesses or Apostles just named." (D&C 107:22-26.)

. . . It should be made clear here that while he [the Patriarch of the Church] has not exercised his authority in a leadership role [such as do the First Presidency and Quorum of the Twelve], that at all times he is recognized in the seating of General Authorities and in the sustaining of General Authorities at General Conference as a prophet, seer and revelator to the Church and that his position comes between that of the Council of the Twelve Apostles and of the First Council of Seventy.[18]

The Position and Responsibility of Stake Patriarchs

Elder John A. Widtsoe stated the position of stake patriarchs in the following manner:

[Stake] patriarchs are especially called and ordained to the work [of giving patriarchal blessings]. Their authority is derived from the President of the Church, in whom the ultimate power of giving such blessings on earth is vested. Their jurisdiction is limited. With the exception of the patriarch to the Church, each is appointed to serve in a limited geographical area, usually a stake in Zion.[19]

In an address to new stake patriarchs, President Harold B. Lee clearly stated who directs the overall ecclesiastical duties of stake patriarchs:

Upon the Council of the Twelve or the traveling high council is placed the responsibility for the selection of and the direction of the work of the patriarchs . . . Make your bond between yourself and the Twelve very close. Ask questions about your own blessings. The Twelve feel a real responsibility.[20]

Of course in directing the duties and responsibilities of stake patriarchs, the members of the Quorum of the Twelve Apostles are acting under the direction and authority of the President of the Church and the First Presidency.[21]

On the stake level, patriarchs "act . . . under the direct supervision of the president of the stake, whose privilege it is to supervise their work and to make adequate provision for it to be carried forward in an orderly way."[22]

It should also be remembered that the office of patriarch is one of blessing, not one of administration. For example, President Spencer W. Kimball has stated:

> The prime duty of the patriarch is to give patriarchal blessings. He was ordained not as a consultant, an administrator, counselor, a financial adviser, or social worker in marital problems. People will be referred to their bishops in these matters. When a patriarch assists in administration of the sick, he does so as an elder and not as a patriarch. And, he does not have the right to forgive sins nor to adjust transgressions. This is the work of the ecclesiastical officers.
>
> It becomes immediately apparent that a patriarch must be an example. He must be worthy, lovable, kind-and since he is the mouthpiece of the Lord in a very special sense, he will desire to live as nearly like the Lord as is possible.[23]

The Preparation of Patriarchs

There is no formal training for newly ordained patriarchs. However, during the past several decades, orientation meetings have been held in Salt Lake City where questions from new patriarchs have been answered by General Authorities.24 Also, the Church has provided small publications to patriarchs which have clarified many aspects of their position[25] and quoted General Authorities on their views of the position and responsibilities of patriarchs.[26]

According to Church leaders, the most effective preparation a patriarch can have in giving patriarchal blessings is "living close to the Lord." For example, President Spencer W. Kimball, speaking to patriarchs on two different occasions, said they were the voice of the Lord and needed to live so they could be worthy to be His mouthpiece:

> I suppose you are the voice of the Lord as few people of the Church are and therefore you should be the closest men in the world to the Lord. I believe every patriarch must realize that in giving blessings he himself has no blessing to give but he is the mouthpiece of the Lord, and if he will keep himself in tune then the Lord will send a message through him. The patriarch is in a position to make friends with everyone. There is no need of having anything but the best of feelings. You are in a position where you can always give blessings, but never need to criticize because it is only those who are righteous that come to you. They have already been screened by the bishop.
>
> You stand out high in the estimate of the people. You should see that every thought of your life is high. Every action in your life should be holy.

Your thoughts should be in keeping with the Spirit of the Lord.[27]

In a real sense, your voice is to give utterance to the message of the Lord which he has in store for the individuals who come to you. You are not the source of the promises; you have no blessings for anyone; you are but the tube through which the blessings flow—the wire through which the promises are carried. You must be sure that you do not arrogate to yourselves any of these powers. One of the most important qualities for a patriarch to possess is that of humility. . . .[28]

And President Joseph Fielding Smith has said:

In all humility the patriarch should approach his task in the spirit of faith and prayer, that he might have the guidance of the Spirit of the Lord to declare upon the heads of those who receive blessings the things that are best suited for them to guide them and direct them through this life.[29]

Similarly, President Harold B. Lee has stated that a patriarch's first responsibility is "to prepare [himself] to give blessings. . . . The Lord can best speak through a man who is prepared . . . then the next thing to do is humble [himself] to get the Spirit."[30]

A Church publication has suggested another way that a patriarch can prepare himself to give patriarchal blessings which might also be appropriate for those who are preparing to receive—or have already received—their patriarchal blessing:

Gain a thorough knowledge of the gospel. Learn about the patriarchal office. Study the lives of the prophets and patriarchs, the lineage of Abraham and his successors, the tribes of Israel and their mission and promises. Learn the covenants of the gospel and their meanings, the eternal principles of the plan of salvation, and the gifts of the spirit as outlined in section 46 of the Doctrine and Covenants, chapter 10 of Moroni, and chapter 12 of 1 Corinthians.[31]

The Two Types of Patriarchs: Ordained and Natural

In the Church we have two types of patriarchs: an "ordained patriarch" and a "natural patriarch." The "ordained patriarch" we call a "patriarch."[32] He holds a specific office in the Melchizedek Priesthood and, as such, the Patriarch to the Church as well as all stake patriarchs are considered "ordained patriarchs." Regarding "ordained patriarchs," President Joseph Fielding Smith has said:

> Patriarchs who are ordained have sealed upon their heads the right of revelation—prophecy so that they can have, if they seek for the guidance of the Spirit of the Lord, the right and authority to pronounce upon the heads of those who receive the blessings things pertaining to their good by prophecy and revelation. They also have the right to seal upon those who receive these blessings the privilege of coming forth on the morning of the first resurrection, based of course, upon their faithfulness.[33]

In comparison to an "ordained patriarch," a "natural patriarch" is the father in any home

whether he is a member of the Church or not.
Elder Eldred G. Smith has stated: "If that father
doesn't hold the priesthood, he is still the 'patriarch' of his family and has the right to take care
of the functions pertaining to any of the activities
of his own home":

> We have in the Church two kinds of patriarchs.
> . . . There are the natural fathers, or natural patri-
> archs . . . a father and a patriarch are used syn-
> onymously in this sense. Then there are those
> who are ordained patriarchs, which is an office of
> Priesthood. So we say the father in the home is the
> patriarch in his own home, even though he holds
> no Priesthood or is not even a member of the
> Church he is still the patriarch in his own home.
> He is the father in his own home. So, as a natur-
> al father, he has the right to take care of any of the
> functions pertaining to any of the activities of his
> own home. Now, priesthood is of a patriarchal
> order. That means the order of the fathers. If a
> man is an ordained patriarch then he holds an
> office in the Priesthood by virtue of ordination
> which is that of father or of giving father's bless-
> ings. . . . If he is a member of the Church and
> holds the Priesthood, then he may bless his chil-
> dren by virtue of the Priesthood which he holds,
> which gives it that much more authenticity and
> more right in giving a blessing. If a man is a hold-
> er of the Aaronic Priesthood, then he has the right
> to perform the functions of the Aaronic Priesthood
> to the members of his family. That's Patriarchal
> Order. If he is an Elder, then he has a right to per-
> form those functions of the Priesthood to the

members of his family pertaining to the office of Elder or Melchizedek Priesthood.[34]

So the father in any home is the "natural patriarch" of that home since the two words are basically synonymous. As the "patriarch" of his family, a father may bless his family members, and he can and should pray for his family and for himself as the head of his family. But unless that father holds the priesthood, he has no valid authority with which to administer a blessing through "the power and authority of God delegated to man on earth."[35] (The specific differences between an ordained patriarch's blessing and a father's blessing are discussed in Chapter 2 of this book.)

Some members of the Church are in a rather unique situation in that their natural and ordained patriarch is the same person, namely, their own earthly father. Elder LeGrand Richards was in this situation. He relates the following experience:

> When I was called on my first mission I walked into the office of Brother George Reynolds on crutches, with my leg in a plaster cast. He said: "What are you here for?" I said: "I am here to answer a call for a mission." He said: "It looks to me like you had better go home and take care of yourself." I said: "I will be ready to go at the appointed date." He said: "When do you want to go?" I said: "In April, with my other friends." That was in February.
>
> I went out to Tooele, where my father lived, a patriarch of God. I told him I wanted a blessing so

I could go on that mission, and my father promised me that I should go and that I should not be handicapped because of lameness-and I never lost a day's work. I threw my crutches away a few days before it was time to leave, and I went on that mission.[36]

Those members of the Church who do not have a stake patriarch for a natural father are certainly in the majority, while those who have fathers who are stake patriarchs usually realize the blessings of being able to closely associate with one of the Lord's mouthpieces here on earth.

However, every member of the Church can partake of the patriarch's spirit by getting a patriarchal blessing from an ordained patriarch of the Church.

Notes to Chapter 1

1. Bruce R. McConkie, *Mormon Doctrine* (Salt Lake City: Bookcraft,1966), p. 558.
2. Eldred G. Smith, "Lectures in Theology: Last Message Series" (Salt Lake Institute of Religion, April 30, 1971), p. 2.
3. Joseph Smith, *Teachings of the Prophet Joseph Smith* (Deseret Book Company,1939), p.151.
4. LeGrand Richards, *Patriarchal Blessings* (address to BYU Studentbody, May 27,1953), p.2.
5. Calvin McOmber, Jr., *The Historical Development of the Patriarchal Priesthood* (History of Religion 645, BYU, 1979), pp. 58-59.
6. Thomas W. Grassley, *Answers to Questions About Patriarchal Blessings* (Springville: 1979), pp. 58-59.

7. *Ibid.*
8. 1981 *Church Almanac* (Deseret News, 1980), pp. 6, 95, 113,116.
9. Bruce R. McConkie, *op. cit.*, p. 558.
10. John Taylor, *Patriarchal* (Times and Seasons, June 1, 1845, Number 6), p. 921.
11. John A. Widtsoe, "What Is the Meaning of Patriarchal Blessings?" Address to stake presidencies of BYU stakes, 1965, p. 3. (See also *Improvement Era*, January,1942.)
12. John A. Widtsoe, *Priesthood and Church Government* (Salt Lake City: Deseret Book,1939), p.270.
13. *Ibid.*, p . 247.
14. R. Clayton Brough, *Statements from Church Publications about Patriarchal Blessings* (West Valley City, Utah: 1983), p.1.
15. *Ibid.*, p. 1.
16. Bruce R. McConkie, *op. cit.*, p.561.
17. R. Clayton Brough,1983, *op. cit.*, p.1.
18. Thomas Jay Kemp, *The Office of Patriarch to The Church* (Monograph pub. at Stanford, Connecticut: 1972), pp.6-9.
19. John A. Widtsoe,1965, *op. cit.*, p.2.
20. R. Clayton Brough,1983, *op. cit.*, p. 2.
21. R. Clayton Brough,1983, *op. cit.*, p.1-2.
22. R. Clayton Brough,1983, *op. cit.*, p. 3.
23. Spencer W. Kimball, "Comments to Patriarchs" (meeting of Church patriarchs), Oct. 3,1969.
24. Example of earlier meetings: Apr. 7, 1956, and Oct. 11, 1958.
25. R. Clayton Brough,1983, *op. cit.*, p.1.
26. *Ibid.*, p. 2-3.
27. *Ibid.*, p.2.
28. Spencer W. Kimball,1969, *op. cit.*

29. Joseph Fielding Smith, "Address of Joseph Fielding Smith" (BYU Church History and Philosophy 245), June 15, 1956, p. 5.
30. R. Clayton Brough, 1983, *op. cit.*, p. 2.
31. *Ibid.*, p.1.
32. *Ibid.*, p.3.
33. Joseph Fielding Smith, 1956, *op. cit.*, p.3.
34. Eldred G. Smith, "Patriarchal Blessings," Salt Lake Institute of Religion, Jan.17,1964, p.1.
35. Bruce R. McConkie, *op. cit.*, pp. 594-595.
36. LeGrand Richards, *Conference Report*, Oct. 6, 1939, p.25.

2

The Definition of a Patriarchal Blessing

Defining "Patriarchal Blessings"

On June 28, 1957, the First Presidency of the Church (comprised of David O. McKay, Stephen L. Richards, and J. Reuben Clark, Jr.) gave the following definition of "patriarchal blessings":

> Patriarchal blessings contemplate an inspired declaration of the lineage of the recipient, and also where so moved upon by the spirit, an inspired and prophetic statement of the life mission of the recipient, together with such blessings, cautions, and admonitions as the patriarch may be prompted to give for the accomplishment of such life's mission, it being always made clear that the realization of all promised blessings is conditioned upon faithfulness to the gospel of our Lord, whose servant the patriarch is.[1]

And Elder John A. Widtsoe has stated that:

A patriarchal blessing . . . promises the members [of the Church] blessings which are in store for them, on earth and in heaven, which are sealed upon them on conditions of obedience to the law of the Lord; it confers power upon us, if we will use it, to win the fulfillment of these promises, as we journey through life; and special blessings are made available to us to meet our daily needs.[2]

The Difference Between Patriarchal Blessings and Other Blessings

The three main factors that separate a patriarchal blessing from most other priesthood blessings are: (1) a patriarchal blessing is officially the *only* blessing in which our lineage is declared by an ordained patriarch; (2) it is the *only* blessing recorded and sent to the Church Historian's office; and (3) it *usually* contains sealing blessings concerning the resurrection (which is discussed in Chapter 4 of this book).

Other blessings—such as a father's blessing, blessing the sick, and a blessing of comfort—also utilize the priesthood through the laying on of hands, but they are not usually concerned with our lineage or matters concerning the resurrection, nor are they sent to and officially retained by the Church Historian's office. It would not be practical to file the millions of other blessings given each year by members of the Church. For example, Elder John A. Widtsoe has written:

So important are these official patriarchal blessings that they should always be reduced to writing and preserved. Every blessing is entered upon the record of the patriarch and ultimately deposited with the Church historian. The person blessed receives a copy of the blessing for his use and comfort.[3]

And President Joseph Fielding Smith has stated:

According to [the] patriarchal order, every faithful man in the Church who holds the Melchizedek Priesthood is a patriarch to his own family. He may give blessings to his own children, but his blessings will not be recorded and filed in the archives of the Church. He may record them if he wishes in his own records; but these blessings are not sent to the Historian's Office nor filed Every blessing that is given by a patriarch who is ordained to serve in a stake of Zion, is filed in the Historian's Office to be preserved through the generations of time.[4]

In addition, Elder Joseph F. Smith has said the following in answer to the question: "Are fathers entitled to give their children patriarchal blessings?"

The answer is yes and no. After all, if you are going to deal technically merely in the meanings of words, a patriarchal blessing means a father's blessing. A patriarch is literally a paternal ruler. That is what the word means, and any father in the Church who holds the higher priesthood may, in the authority of that priesthood give unto his child a blessing, and that is a patriarchal blessing in that it is a father's blessing.

But according to the ruling of the Church, that blessing is not to be recorded as having come from an ordained patriarch, because it does not come from an ordained patri arch. The business of declaring lineage and giving patriarchal blessings—these blessings given by one who is ordained a patriarch—that is the privilege of the ordained patriarch. Such blessings are recorded and kept in the Church historian's library.[5]

As Elder Smith stated above, a father can give his family members a patriarchal blessing, but as mentioned before. there are usually three significant differences between patriarchal blessings given by natural fathers and those given by ordained patriarchs. Therefore, it would be best for all members of the Church to receive one patriarchal blessing from an ordained patriarch, then have a father or other priesthood holder administer other blessings as needed.

Receiving a father's blessing does have one major advantage over a patriarchal blessing given by an ordained patriarch, and that is that one can have a father's blessing as many times as needed or desired. For example, President Spencer W. Kimball has stated:

Of course, it is the right of every father and his duty as patriarch of his own family to give a father's blessing to his children, and it is our hope that every father will give a sacred blessing to each of his children, especially as they are leaving home to go to school or on missions or to be married, which blessing should then be noted in the individual's private journal.[6]

Similarly, Elder Eldred G. Smith has said this about "a father's blessing":

Now, you young people, every time you have a change in life, some new venture in life, then you should go to your father (if he holds the Melchizedek Priesthood) and claim a Father's Blessing. In addition to that you should have at least one blessing by an ordained patriarch. I can tell you families where the children have all received a blessing from their Stake Patriarch and in addition they have all received blessings from their father which he has recorded, for a family record. They received a blessing from their father when they got married. They received a blessing from their father when they left to go on their mission, and some when they returned from their mission, and other boys when they left to go into the service. These are similar occasions that I'm referring to . . . new ventures in life which require or set the stage for a request for a Father's Blessing from your own father. These can be recorded for your own records. Now, people in the mission field can do the same thing. Or they can go to their Branch President or the Mission President to receive a blessing; but in these cases the declaration of lineage and the sealing blessing and the recording in the Church Archives will be omitted. But all the rest which might go into a Patriarchal Blessing can be given by these other men holding the Priesthood; or the Father who is the natural Patriarch, holding the Melchizedek Priesthood, can give those blessings.[7]

In another instance, Elder Smith related how a husband and wife benefited from "a real father's blessing":

I remember another occasion. A lady came in wanting a special blessing, but she didn't want to tell me—in fact, she wouldn't tell me why she wanted a blessing. She felt that I should be able to tell her why she wanted a blessing. This is no joke. People do that repeatedly. They think I can tell them everything about their life, everything about their future. I don't have that kind of a crystal ball. The more I talked to this lady the more I decided that if she wasn't going to tell me why she wanted the blessing I couldn't see why I should give her a blessing. How can I give her a blessing unless I bless her for something, and I couldn't find out what the blessing was to be for? I did find out in the discussion that her husband was a holder of the Melchizedek Priesthood, so after explaining patriarchal blessings to her for an hour and a half or more she left my office. 1 thought I had done a pretty good job explaining priesthood authority, etc. A few months later she came back to my office and said, reminding me of the experience, "I left your office very resentful that day." And I thought I had done a good job. 1 wondered what went wrong. Then she said, "That is one of the finest things that has ever happened in our family." So I had to have the rest of the story. She told me that the reason she wanted a blessing was that she and her husband had been at odds with each other. There hadn't been the harmony in the home that there should have been and I had told her to go back to her husband and have him give her a blessing. Naturally she was resentful. Nevertheless, this was a two-sided situation. She had to do some repenting, and he had to do some repenting. She thought it over for a long time, she said, and prayed about it, and finally must have gotten enough courage to ask her husband for the blessing. It shocked him, of course. She gave him time to think it over and get over the shock and finally he gave her the blessing. What happened was that he repented and she repented, and he sealed upon her head the blessing that they had both earned. She said, "There has never been such a pleasant relationship in our home in all our married life as there has been since he gave me that blessing." This is a real father's blessing; this is how we properly put it into effect. You have problems and you work it out together, you get an answer, don't you?[8]

The Difference Between Patriarchal Blessings and Fortunetelling

A survey conducted in the 1970s indicated that some young people and some converts to the Church believed that fortunetelling and patriarchal blessings were very similar. In essence, these church members felt that "fortune-tellers tell you what's going to happen in your future, and so do patriarchs."[9]

Elder Eldred G. Smith has stated that "fortunetelling and patriarchal blessings are as far apart as light and darkness," because fortunetelling consists of predictions of predestined events—which is the doctrine and work of Satan, while patriarchal blessings reveal blessings which our Father in Heaven would like us to receive and which we may earn through obedience:

> The blessings of the priesthood are not fortunetelling. Fortunetelling boils down to Satan's doctrine because fortunetelling is predicting what is going to happen. That is predestination, and predestination is Satan's doctrine, just the complete opposite from the blessings from the Lord. We have to earn the blessings [from the Lord] or we don't get them.[10]

> Too often people get the idea that when they go to the ordained patriarch, he has some special power and that he can take out of an imaginary pigeonhole a special blessing that is for them. Some hold that he or any other patriarch at any time in their lives can reach in and get that one particular blessing and that it will be the same identical one, word for word, if a second one is given. That is not so.

> In other words, that is putting it down to the point of predestination—that we are given the promise of what will come [without choice on the part of the individual or without regard of what the individual does or does not do]. There is no such thing as predestination in the Gospel of Jesus Christ. Predestination is linked with fortunetelling. Fortunetelling and patriarchal blessings are as far apart as light and darkness, as black and white. There is no relationship between a patriarchal blessing and fortunetelling. Fortunetelling is a declaration of what will happen,

which implies predestination; and predestination is Satan's doctrine.[11]

In addition, Elder John A. Widtsoe has similarly stated that patriarchal blessings are possibilities "predicated upon faithful devotion":

> These [patriarchal] blessings are possibilities predicated upon faithful devotion to the cause of truth. They must be earned. Otherwise they are but empty words. Indeed, they rise to their highest value when used as ideals, specific possibilities, towards which we may strive throughout life. To look upon a patriarch as a fortuneteller is an offense to the Priesthood; the patriarch only indicates the gifts the Lord would give us, if we labor for them. He helps us by pointing out the divine goal which we may enjoy if we pay the price.[12]

And President Joseph Fielding Smith has remarked:

> I say a patriarchal blessing is not fortunetelling, but many times the patriarch will pronounce upon the head of the individual some blessing based upon his faithfulness which may be fulfilled. I know of one or two cases of that kind where a brother has been blessed by the patriarch and told that he would become a member of the Council of the Twelve. Usually they don't say that, no one says that, even if the patriarch felt that the chances are that a man would be called to the leading councils of the Church. [But], I want to tell you of this story of Alonzo A. Hinckley . . . who presided in the Deseret Stake for a number of years. He received a blessing, and in that blessing

the patriarch said that the time would come when he would be ordained and placed in the Council of the Twelve. Brother Hinckley said to himself: "That's an impossibility." He took his blessing and put it away and said, "I became disappointed; I knew it couldn't be fulfilled; I lost my faith in the patriarch, and my blessing did not serve me as it should have done." Well [later], Alonzo A. Hinckley was called into the Council of the Twelve.

Patriarchs should be very careful in giving their blessings not to make extravagant expressions and to be conservative in what they say; but if the Lord does speak to them and tell them to say something, they have that inspiration, and it's their right to say it.[13]

It is also appropriate here to mention that there is no single word-for-word blessing that is one person's blessing alone. Different men phrase things differently, and an individual's circumstances in life can change quite rapidly. However, since all patriarchs require inspiration and revelation to perform their calling, a person could possibly receive the same general blessing from a patriarch in the United States as he could from a patriarch in Japan, because both patriarchs get their inspiration from the same source—the Lord.

Notes to Chapter 2

1. R. Clayton Brough, *Statements from Church Publications about Patriarchal Blessings* (West Valley City, Utah: 1983), p. 2.
2. John A. Widtsoe, "What Is the Meaning of Patriarchal Blessings?" Address to stake presidencies of BYU stakes, 1965, p. 6. (See also Improvement Era, January, 1942.)
3. *Ibid.*, p.2.
4. Joseph Fielding Smith, "Address of Joseph Fielding Smith (BYU Church History and Philosophy 245), June 15, 1956, p. 4.
5. Joseph F. Smith, *Conference Report*, Oct. 7, 1944, pp. 111-112.
6. Spencer W. Kimball, "The Foundations of Righteousness," General Conference, Oct. 1, 1977. (*Ensign*, Nov. 1977, p. 4).
7. Eldred G. Smith, "Patriarchal Blessings," Salt Lake Institute of Religion, Jan. 17,1964, p. 5.
8. Eldred G. Smith, "Lectures in Theology: Last Message Series" (Salt Lake Institute of Religion, April 30,1971), p. 6.
9. Thomas W. Grassley, "Survey on Patriarchal Blessings," Provo, Utah: Sept.-Dec., 1976.
10. Eldred G. Smith, 1971, *op. cit.*, p. 6.
11. Eldred G. Smith, "What Is a Patriarchal Blessing?" (*The Instructor*, Feb. 1962), p. 43.
12. John A. Widtsoe, 1965, *op. cit.*, p. 4.
13. Joseph Fielding Smith, 1956, *op. cit.*, p. 5.

3

The Purpose of a Patriarchal Blessing

The Declaration of Lineage

In 1957, the First Presidency of the Church stated that patriarchal blessings were and are given for two main purposes: (1) to declare through inspiration "the lineage of the recipient," and (2) to "give an inspired and prophetic statement of the life mission of the recipient, together with such blessings, cautions and admonitions as the patriarch may be prompted [through inspiration] to give for the accomplishment of such life's mission, it being always made clear that the realization of all promised blessings are conditioned upon faithfulness to the gospel of our Lord."[1]

With regard to declaring through inspiration "the lineage of the recipient," Elder John A. Widtsoe has said:

In giving a blessing the patriarch may declare our lineage—that is, that we are of Israel, therefore of the family of Abraham, and of a specific tribe of Jacob. In the great majority of cases, Latter-day Saints are of the tribe of Ephraim, the tribe to which has been committed the leadership of the Latter-day work. Whether this lineage is of blood or adoption does not matter (Abraham 2:10). This is very important, for it is through the lineage of Abraham alone that the mighty blessings of the Lord for His children on earth are to be consummated [which include the "blessings" of posterity, eternal increase, leadership through the priesthood, and "blessings of salvation, even of life eternal"; [see Genesis 12:2-3; Abraham 2:9-11; Romans 9:4; Galatians 3:26-29; and D&C 132:28-30].[2]

Regarding the significance of "lineages" that are declared in patriarchal blessings, Elder Eldred G. Smith has stated:

When a person receives a patriarchal blessing, he is entitled to receive a pronouncement of the blessings of Israel, or a declaration of the tribe of Israel through which his blessings shall come. This is the right to the blessings of those recorded in the book of remembrance started in the days of Adam. This does not mean that all nations of the earth will become literal descendants of Abraham, though his seed may be scattered in all nations, but as it says, all shall receive the blessings through those who are the seed of Abraham and shall be accounted his seed, and rise up and bless him as their father (see Abraham 2:10). If members of the Church are literal descendants of Abraham, they will receive such a blessing. If they are not literal descendants of Abraham and join the Church and receive the gospel, they shall receive the priesthood blessings, even eternal life, through those who are of Israel or which would be referred to as by adoption.[3]

We could talk about lineage for a long time. It goes back to the very beginning when Adam's posterity were not following his teachings. Then the Lord gave Adam a promise that he would have posterity that would follow his teachings down through the ends of the earth. Seth was given that promise and the promise was extended down to Noah and from Noah down to Abraham and then to Moses and down to Christ himself and the Apostles. They were given their blessings because of their faithfulness that was started in the days of Adam. So when you come to get a patriarchal blessing, it is the responsibility of the patriarch to designate the line of Israel through which you receive your blessings. These are the choice blessings that make you a part of the Church. You are entitled to this original blessing that was given down through the ages of time, and that you would be a part of this choice lineage.[4]

Now we know that some of the inhabitants of the earth are not descendants of Israel. We know that some of the inhabitants of the earth who join the Church are not direct descendants of Israel . . . yet in the acceptance of the gospel of Jesus Christ they are entitled to the blessings of Israel, and through the power of inspiration the patriarch will assign them to Israel.[5]

A patriarchal blessing, in declaring lineage, does not always need to declare genealogy—it is not a short cut to genealogy. [The patriarch] declares the blessings. Consideration of genealogy may have its effect in assisting the patriarch, but we are mixtures. Many of us are mixtures of several tribes of Israel, and so it is the right of the patriarch to declare that line through which the blessings of Israel shall come. This declaration and the other sealing blessings that are required in a patriarchal blessing are all recorded and filed in the Church archives.[6]

Further information on the "lineages" that are declared in patriarchal blessings is presented in Chapter 7 of this book.

Understanding Who We Are and What We Can Achieve

Besides "declaring through inspiration 'the lineage of the recipient,'" patriarchal blessings are given to "reveal the calling of the Lord unto his children here upon the earth, so that they will have some concept of what the Lord expects of them while they are here in mortality."[7] For example, Elder LeGrand Richards has said:

No doubt many of us in our [patriarchal] blessing have been told that we have not come upon the earth by chance, but in fulfillment of the decree of the Almighty, to perform the mission for which we were foreordained.[8]

[For] you see, those whom God hath chosen before the foundation of the world—and I would like to bear my testimony to you that most of us who were born under the new and everlasting covenant and those of us who have heeded the voice of the messengers of eternal truths and have accepted the same, come under this promise— God has called us out of the world to be his leaders, to be a light unto the world. . . . One of the purposes of patriarchal blessings is to give unto us the inspiration that will enable us to make good here in mortality, that we will be worthy of the great calling that came to us before the foundation of the world [Ephesians 1:1-4; Abraham 3:22-28].[9]

In addition, patriarchal blessings are given to provide members of the Church with their own personal, tangible "guide" or "roadmap"—from which they can prayerfully determine the general direction their life and efforts should follow. For instance, Joseph Smith Sr., the first patriarch of this dispensation, called his family around him when he was on his deathbed, and gave them his final blessing. To his oldest living son, he said: "Hyrum, the only blessing I have for you is to reconfirm upon you your patriarchal blessing which you have already received."[10] This incident led Hyrum G. Smith to say: "This assures me that there is a fundamental principle in a patriarchal blessing when pronounced and recorded. It is an eternal anchor for our soul with the Lord. . . . [And] if you will discover the keynote of your blessing [which may] not be a long one . . . [it will serve as] an index that will point to you . . . the path you should go to serve God and to keep his commandments."[11] Likewise, Elder Eldred G. Smith has stated:

> Patriarchal Blessings are a declaration of accomplishments which you may accomplish if you work hard enough for them. . . . Some people might be having a difficult time getting through school and they go get a Patriarchal Blessing . . . the Patriarch may make some statement as to promise of getting sufficient education to fulfill their purpose in life, their mission in life. Things like that might be given to a person who needs that extra encouragement to cheer them up a little bit and to keep them plugging along because this life's a rough road to go along; it isn't easy. Maybe a person is having physical troubles or financial troubles or he may be headed for them because that might be the very test that the Lord is going to give him. . . .[12]

An Instrument for Encouragement and Comfort

Finally, patriarchal blessings often give repeated courage and comfort to those who receive them- Elder Hyrum G. Smith has said that "thousands of Church members have been kept alive in their devotion to the Church through inspired promises and encouraging counsel and advice given in a patriarchal blessing."[13] And Elder Eldred G. Smith has said:

A patriarchal blessing is much like an anchor to a ship. It is referred to at times as an anchor for your soul, to keep you from being buffeted around. You know what an anchor is to a ship? When the winds rise and the waves come, they drop anchor and that keeps the ship from drifting off course. Well, that is what we need sometimes; is an anchor we can drop in times of emergency, in times of trial, to keep us from drifting off course. Sit down and read your patriarchal blessing, or read a blessing given to you by your father, at a time when you are disturbed, distressed, discouraged and not satisfied with your life. To read your patriarchal blessing sometimes gives you courage and brings you back to where you started from and gets you in the right groove again. It gets your mind set on the proper goals, keeps you from drifting off to one side and going down skid row. It can give you a little extra courage some times when you need it the most.[14]

Indeed, many members of the Church read their patriarchal blessings more often when they are depressed than they do when they are contented. Perhaps the reason for this is that their own "personal scripture"—their patriarchal blessing-seems to smooth out and lessen any troubles they thought were too large before they read their blessing. Knowing that our Heavenly Father cares about each one of us somehow makes insignificant any earthly problems we have been suffering or are facing. For as Elder John A. Widtsoe has said:

A [patriarchal] blessing . . . sealed upon us in the authority of the Priesthood, becomes a power in our lives; a comfort to our days. It is a message which if read an honored aright, will become an anchor in stormy days, of encouragement in cloudy days. It states our certain destination here and hereafter, if we live by the law; and as life goes on, it strengthens our faith and leads us into truth.[15]

Notes to Chapter 3

1. R. Clayton Brough, *Statements from Church Publications about Patriarchal Blessings* (West Valley City, Utah: 1983), p. 2.
2. John A. Widtsoe, "What Is the Meaning of Patriarchal Blessings?" Address to stake presidencies of BYU stakes, 1965, p. 3. (See also *Improvement Era*, Jan.1942.)
   Eldred G. Smith, "Lectures on Theology: Last Message Series," (Salt Lake Institute of Religion, Apr. 30, 1971), p. 2.
   Bruce R. McConkie, *Mormon Doctrine* (Salt Lake City: Bookcraft,1966), pp.13-14.
3. Eldred G. Smith, *Conference Report*, Apr. 6,1971, p.147.
4. Eldred G. Smith, April 30,1971, *op. cit.*, p. 3.
5. Eldred G. Smith, *Conference Report*, Apr. 4, 1952, p. 39.
6. Eldred G. Smith, "Patriarchal Blessings," Salt Lake Institute of Religion, Jan.17,1964, p.42.
7. LeGrand Richards, *Patriarchal Blessings* (address to BYU Studentbody, May 27,1953), p. 5.

8. LeGrand Richards, "A Chosen Vessel Unto Me," (*The Instructor,* Dec.1964), p. 467.
9. LeGrand Richards,1953, *op. cit.,* p. 78.
10. Hyrum G. Smith, *Conference Report,* Apr. 6, 1924, p. 89.
11. *Ibid.,* p. 89.
12. Eldred G. Smith,1964, *op. cit.,* pp. 3-4.
13. Hyrum G. Smith, "Patriarchs and Patriarchal Blessings," (*Improvement Era,* May,1930), p.466.
14. Eldred G. Smith, April 30,1971, *op. cit.,* pp. 6-7.
15. John A. Widtsoe,1965, *op. cit.,* p. 4.

4

The Contents
of a Patriarchal Blessing

What Patriarchal Blessings
Usually Contain

Patriarchal blessings usually contain four general sections: (1) the heading, which contains important historical and genealogical information; (2) an opening that often identifies the authority by which the blessing is being given; (3) the body or general text of the blessing which, through inspiration, identifies the lineage of the recipient and gives other blessings, promises, advice, admonitions and warnings as the patriarch may be prompted by the Spirit to give to the recipient; and (4) a closing, which often contains "sealing blessings."

The Heading of Patriarchal Blessings

Today, the heading of patriarchal blessings contains important historical and genealogical information. When a recipient goes to obtain his or her patriarchal blessing, the patriarch giving the blessing will complete the heading of the blessing by listing his own name (as the patriarch who gave the blessing), the recipient's name, the name of his or her mother and father, the stake and ward in which the recipient resides and the date the blessing is given.

According to Elder Hyrum G. Smith, these historical and genealogical facts were not always contained in the heading of patriarchal blessings:

> No dates or formal genealogy were given [in the early days of the Church], but in later generations came the time for more formal and detailed genealogies, including the time and place of the blessing.[1]

The Opening of Patriarchal Blessings

When he is giving a person a patriarchal blessing, the patriarch lays his hands on the head of the recipient and calls him or her by name. He often begins his blessing by identifying the authority through which he is giving the blessing. The necessity for the patriarch to state the authority through which he is acting is explained in the following statement which appeared in a Church publication:

> As with all other priesthood blessings, the patriarchal blessing is given by the authority of the priesthood and in the name of Jesus Christ; and at some point in the blessing, in the natural

words of the patriarch, this authority should be acknowledged.[2]

The Body or General Text of Patriarchal Blessings

As stated in Chapter 2 of this book, the First Presidency of the Church has stated that the body or general text of patriarchal blessings (which normally constitutes the largest section of patriarchal blessings) usually contains or contemplates:

> . . . An inspired declaration of the lineage of the recipient, and also where so moved upon by the Spirit, an inspired and prophetic statement of the life mission of the recipient, together with such blessings, cautions, and admonitions as the patriarch may be prompted to give for the accomplishment of such life's mission, it being always made clear that the realization of all promised blessings is conditional upon faithfulness to the gospel of our Lord, whose servant the Patriarch is. . . .[3]

In relation to the above statement, several General Authorities have made similar remarks when talking about what is contained in patriarchal blessings. For example, Elder Hyrum G. Smith has stated:

> . . . The body of the blessing . . . contains sacred promises, for comfort, or for counsel, or warning; pointing to certain possibilities of blessings, always predicated upon obedience to natural laws and faithfulness. It also should contain the declaration of lineage; that is, the tribe in Israel in

which, or through which, the promises of inheritance shall come, even as assignments of the inheritances to ancient Israel.[4]

And President Spencer W. Kimball has said:

In each blessing, the patriarch will declare, under inspiration, the literal blood lineage of the person to be blessed and then, as moved upon by the Spirit, make a statement as to the possibilities and the special spiritual gifts, cautions, instructions, admonitions and warnings as the patriarch may be prompted to give. . . .[5]

Also, Elder Eldred G. Smith has stated:

A patriarchal blessing is usually about one page, sometimes more or less, of typewritten statements. It is impossible in that short time to give the outline or blueprint of all that is going to happen in our lives. It is a record of the outstanding things which might happen if we put forth a little extra effort and faithfulness and seek the guidance of the Lord a little bit more, usually that which might be hardest for us to accomplish.[6]

And Elder S. Dilworth Young has said:

The stake patriarch has the power to (1) declare your lineage in the house of Israel; (2) seal you to come forth in the first resurrection if you are faithful; (3) remind you of weaknesses you possess and warn you against them; and (4) prophesy some of the events in your future in this life.[7]

In addition, a Church publication states that:

To the extent that the Spirit directs, the patriarch should identify for the recipient work to be done, accomplishments to be realized, challenges to be overcome, and blessings to be received, reminding always that promises and gospel blessings from the Lord are contingent on faithful, worthy living. [Also] patriarchal blessings give encouragement to keep the commandments and to qualify for eternal life, and help to define responsibilities and goals.[8]

The Closing of Patriarchal Blessings

The closing part of patriarchal blessings usually contains "sealing blessings" concerning the resurrection. Regarding these blessings, Elder Eldred G. Smith has stated:

> The closing of a blessing is the sacred sealing of the Holy Melchizedek Priesthood. The blessing pronounced, with all it contains, should serve as a comfort and guide through life according to faithfulness and is sealed forever upon the conditions of faithfulness to the laws of God, which includes the laws of nature.[9]

> Patriarchal blessings should, in addition to the lineage, give you the sealing blessings—blessings of coming forth in the first resurrection. We could talk a lot about the resurrection, of what the morning of the first resurrection is [and] what the first resurrection is. We don't need to worry about the others because we don't want them. The only one that we should have a goal for is the morning of the first resurrection, which is exaltation and can be had only by the sealing blessings of husband and wife for time and eternity. The first res-

urrection is celestial, which includes all three divisions within the celestial.[10]

Also, Elder John A. Widtsoe has said:

Then, the patriarch, looking into the future, enumerates the blessings and promises, some special, others general, to which the person of the proper lineage, who receives the blessings, is entitled; and through his authority seals them upon him [or her] so that they may be his [or hers] forever through faithfulness.[11]

Scriptural Examples of Patriarchal Blessings

Because of the sacredness of patriarchal blessings, the authors of this book have decided *not* to include latter-day examples of such blessings. Instead, the authors wish to refer the reader to those examples already contained in scripture: see Genesis 49; 2 Nephi 1:28-32, 2:1-3, 3:1-4, 3:25, 4:3-12.

Notes to Chapter 4

1. Hyrum G. Smith, "Patriarchs and Patriarchal Blessings," (Improvement Era, May,1930), p.466.
2. R. Clayton Brough, *Statements from Church Publications about Patriarchal Blessings* (West Valley City, Utah: 1983), p.1.
3. See Chapter 2 of this book.
4. Hyrum G. Smith,1930, *op. cit.*, p. 466.
5. Spencer W. Kimball, "Comments to Patriarchs" (meeting of Church patriarchs, Oct. 3, 1969), quoted in *The Teachings of Spencer W. Kimball*, (Bookcraft,1982), p. 43.
6. Eldred G. Smith, "What Is a Patriarchal Blessing?" (*The Instructor*, Feb.1962), p. 43.
7. S. Dilworth Young, *Family Night Reader, A Young Peoples' Guide in Gospel Study*, Salt Lake City: Bookcraft, 1958, p.133.
8. R. Clayton Brough,1983, *op. cit.*, p.1.
9. Eldred G. Smith, *Conference Report*, Apr. 4, 1952, p. 39.
10. Eldred G. Smith, "Lectures in Theology: Last Message Series" (Salt Lake Institute of Religion, April 30, 1971), p. 7.
11. John A. Widtsoe, "What Is the Meaning of Patriarchal Blessings?" Address to stake presidencies of BYU stakes, 1965, p. 3. (See also *Improvement Era*, Jan.1942.)

5

Preparing for a Patriarchal Blessing

Patriarchal Blessings Are for All Church Members

Although patriarchal blessings "may not be necessary for salvation," they do contain inspired words of counsel and guidance that recipients can refer to "whenever needed in the darkness and in the storm" of life. For example, President Spencer W. Kimball has stated:

> The patriarchal blessing may not be necessary for salvation, but it is a guidepost; a white line down the middle of the road; a series of stakes around the mountain pass with reflector buttons in them so that whenever needed in the darkness and in the storm, they are available. . . . Every boy and girl may be encouraged to prepare for [a patriarchal blessing] but never urged or forced to obtain their patriarchal blessing. Certainly these blessings should never be used to fill a require-

ment to achieve an award. It is a blessing for which young people should be adequately prepared, morally, mentally and spiritually.[1]

Throughout the history of the Church, General Authorities have often encouraged all Latter-day Saints to obtain their patriarchal blessings. For instance, in the early 1940s, Elder John A. Widtsoe wrote that "All Church members may claim the patriarchal blessings flowing from their membership in the assemblage of families within the Church";[2] and in 1977, President Spencer W. Kimball stated: "It is our great hope that every person. including the older youth, will be given the opportunity of having a patriarchal blessing, which is recorded in the official records of the Church."[3]

Sometimes, LDS parents who have children that are mentally or physically handicapped ask Church leaders if such children can receive patriarchal blessings. The two examples that follow provide the answer to this question:

> In a patriarch's meeting in Salt Lake City, one patriarch asked President Joseph Fielding Smith about a mentally handicapped person in his stake. She was an adult, but possessed the mental capacity of a child, and her family wanted to know if she could receive a patriarchal blessing. President Smith answered: "For her sake, I don't know why a patriarch would not give her a blessing. It may give her some comfort. Her condition is something which is not eternal. That is a physical condition that will disappear in the resurrection. I don't know why a blessing could not be given to

such a person, although the mental capacity is only that of a child.[4]

In another instance, one patriarch received a request for a patriarchal blessing from a seventeen-year-old boy who had leukemia and who was not expected to live very long. The patriarch asked President Harold B. Lee what he should do, and President Lee stated that since patriarchal blessings are of an eternal nature that the patriarch should "go right ahead and give [the boy] his blessing as it is revealed to you." The patriarch gave the boy a blessing and soon afterward the young man died. However, both his parents expressed the great comfort they received as they read over their son's blessing and better understood the eternal nature of man.[5]

Patriarchal blessings are only given by patriarchs to LDS Church members. As Eldred G. Smith has explained: "We don't give patriarchal blessings to nonmembers. They have to be a member of the Church and then they become eligible to receive the blessings of the Priesthood. . . . They have to accept [the Gospel] before they can get the blessings of the Gospel."[6]

When to Receive a Patriarchal Blessing

Church leaders and patriarchs have often discussed the problems of giving patriarchal blessings to Church members who are either too young to "understand the meaning and purpose . . . of a patriarchal blessing," or too old where "opportunity for [further mortal] service is very limited." For example, President Joseph Fielding Smith

discouraged giving patriarchal blessings "to small
children who cannot understand what they are,"
for sometimes such a child grows to adulthood
and is "not satisfied and wants another blessing."[7] Also, Elder Eldred G. Smith has stated that
before a "child" should receive a patriarchal
blessing, he or she should be old enough to
understand the "purpose and meaning" and
value of a patriarchal blessing, and not because
an adult or parent has the desire that the child
should receive a blessing.[8]

Concerning the elderly, Elder Smith once told
of "giving a man a patriarchal blessing who was
in his nineties, and before . . . the blessing [was]
transcribed and mailed to him, he died." All that
Elder Smith could give the older man were "general statements" and "commendations for his
past life," for the man's "life [was] fixed" and his
"opportunity for [further mortal] service [was]
very limited."[9]

In addition, Elder Smith comments as to when
members of the Church might consider obtaining
their patriarchal blessings:

> I definitely discourage anyone . . . receiving
> their blessings from an ordained Patriarch before
> they are twelve years of age. If I were a Stake Patri-
> arch I would raise the age a little above that. . . . I
> think the age between fifteen and twenty-five is
> the best age. Of course, that depends on the indi-
> vidual. It should be at a time when you want the
> blessing; not when the class group is going to get
> their blessings or not when your neighbor or your
> friend or your buddy is going to get a blessing . . .

but when you, yourself, personally feel that you want a blessing from an ordained Patriarch, and this is the only one you are going to get in your life, to be on record for this occasion, for this kind of blessing . . . that's the time for you to go get your blessing. That isn't a split second timing, that's a general timing.[10]

It should come at a time when the individual has a desire to be of service to others, when he has a desire to do the work which the Lord desires of him. He should be old enough to understand the history of Israel and the blessings of Israel. He should be of an age when he begins to feel the "loosening of his mother's apron strings" and has the desire to make something of himself in serving the Lord in this life.[11]

Missionaries & Patriarchal Blessings

In 1921, Elder Hyrum G. Smith stated:

I see hundreds of young men as they go out from their homes into the world, to carry the message of life and salvation to the world. Under the duties of my office I am enabled to admonish these young men, to give them a blessing, which, with their faith and their works, the Lord is able to bring to pass a fulfillment of the promise or promises [given to them], and they go out to all the world, in all the nations of the world where the gospel door is open, they have faith in the promises given and they live by them, and they come back and testify that the blessings have been a source of strength and power to them. Others go out into the world without the blessing; and many of them have written to me in this manner:

"Brother Smith, here am 1, away over in Liverpool; I am on a mission; I was unable to get my blessing when I went away from home, and now I am over here in the service of the Lord; my companions have blessings and they receive comfort from them; can't you send me a blessing, 1 need a blessing, can't you write one, and send it to me?" Well, 1 have to send word to them that I can pray for them, and when they come home, then I can officiate for them in the regular way and give them a blessing. And so I admonish the young elders, the missionaries, both men and women, to get their blessings before they leave home, so that they will have these comforts and guides in their missionary experiences abroad.[12]

In 1971, Elder Eldred G. Smith said:

. . . I think ofttimes young men get a patriarchal blessing before they go on their missions because they think that is part of the program of going on a mission, but often when they get back from their mission is when they need a blessing. They get a blessing when they are set apart to go on a mission, that should take care of him and give him a guide to work toward; but when they come back they are dropped from all of their intensive activity of missionary work. He has to get back into college or school or vocation or prepare himself for the rest of his life. He has been going at a heavy pace and now the whole program changes for him. This might be a better time for a patriarchal blessing.[13]

Therefore, based on these two statements, prospective missionaries should give serious thought and prayer about "when" they should obtain a patriarchal blessing. In addition, a 1978 Church publication states:

> Ordinarily, missionaries receive their patriarchal blessings before reporting for missionary service. A missionary who did not receive his patriarchal blessing, may, when properly recommended by the mission president, receive his blessing from a stake patriarch in the area.[14]

The Steps in Obtaining a Patriarchal Blessing

Before receiving a patriarchal blessing from an ordained patriarch, members of the Church should be aware that there are several steps that should or must be taken by them preparatory to receiving their patriarchal blessing. A Church publication states:

> It is quite important that candidates for blessings prepare themselves for reception of that which the Lord has in store for them. Selfish motives or desires should find no place in their thoughts as they seek the Lord's blessing through His servant. They should under no circumstance regard patriarchal blessings as a matter of fortunetelling. Clean hands and a pure heart may well be their guiding objective. Humility and willing submission to the Lord's will will surely merit His divine approval. Parents may be instructed to teach their children respecting these virtues, while bishops and stake presidents may well inform adult members, who seek blessings, respecting such matters.[15]

In addition, Church publications have outlined necessary steps candidates for patriarchal blessings should take before they receive their blessing:

1. Keep the commandments so as to merit the blessings of the Lord.
2. Study the gospel and learn the nature and purpose of such blessings.
3. Petition the Lord [through prayer] to give inspiration to the patriarch.
4. Have sufficient maturity in the Church to understand and appreciate the significance of the blessing.
5. [After having an interview with your bishop (or branch president, stake president or mission president—as the situation may necessitate)] make an appointment with the patriarch [to receive a blessing].[16]

Regarding these steps and suggestions, Elder John A. Widtsoe has written that "those who seek patriarchal blessings should . . . be qualified to receive their blessings by conformity in their lives to the requirements of the gospel":

> Those who seek patriarchal blessings should ask for them with faith in the reality of the power of the Priesthood. They should seek them with an earnest, prayerful desire to become, through the blessings, more completely happy in their lives, and more perfectly serviceable in the work of the Lord. And they should, of course, be qualified to receive their blessings by conformity in their lives to the requirements of the gospel. The unclean or

disobedient person should cleanse himself, and learn obedience before going to the patriarch. Only under such conditions can a person expect to learn of the will of the Lord.[17]

Also, President Spencer W. Kimball has stated:

Everything reasonable should be done to keep the program [of giving and receiving patriarchal blessings] dignified. Parents should teach their children the dignity and power of this program, which is unique in all the world. The recipient may wish to fast in anticipation of the blessing and to especially pray for the patriarch that the blessing the Lord had in his heart would be received. The children would not usually come in groups nor would a blessing be given to fill a requirement for other activities. It is never given to satisfy curiosity or cheap interests. It is of prime importance itself and should be surrounded with cautions and protections. The patriarch will not solicit blessings, but the bishop and stake presidency may teach and stir the people to anticipate these great privileges.[18]

And President Joseph F. Smith has said:

A patriarchal blessing is a very personal thing. Sometimes zealous teachers in auxiliary organizations develop enthusiasm in classes for patriarchal blessings, and there have been cases where whole classes have gone to receive their patriarchal blessings at one time. This . . . would better be avoided. It is commendable, on the part of teachers of children, to talk about patriarchal blessings, to explain the importance of them and their value, but the individual himself, if he wants it, should first obtain his proper recommendation, and then make his own appointment with the patriarch, and having received that blessing he should hold it sacred. It is not a thing to be published; it is not for everybody to see; it is for his comfort, for his strengthening. It is his blessing.[19]

Notes to Chapter 5

1. Spencer W. Kimball, "The Ordinances of the Gospel," Seminary and Institute Teachers, BYU, June 18,1962.
2. John A. Widtsoe, "What Is the Meaning of Patriarchal Blessings?" Address to stake presidencies of BYU stakes, 1965, p.2. (See also *Improvement Era,* January 1942.)
3. Spencer W. Kimball, *Conference Report,* October 1, 1977.
4. Thomas W. Grassley, *Answers to Questions About Patriarchal Blessings* (Springville: 1979), pp. 16-17.
5. *Ibid.*
6. Eldred G. Smith, "Lectures in Theology: Last Message Series" (Salt Lake Institute of Religion, April 30, 1971), p. 4.
7. R. Clayton Brough, *Statements from Church Publications about Patriarchal Blessings* (West Valley City, Utah: 1983), p.2.
8. Eldred G. Smith, "What Is a Patriarchal Blessing?" (*The Instructor,* Feb. 1962), p.43;
   Eldred G. Smith, "Patriarchal Blessings," Salt Lake Institute of Religion, January 17,1964, p.6.
9. Eldred G. Smith, 1964, *op. cit.,* p. 6.

10. *Ibid.*
11. Eldred G. Smith, 1962, *op. cit.*, p. 43.
12. Hyrum G. Smith, *Conference Report,* April 6,1921, p.186.
13. Eldred G. Smith, 1971, *op. cit.*, p. 4-5.
14. R. Clayton Brough, 1983, *op. cit.*, p. 1.
15. *Ibid.*, p.2.
16. *Ibid.*, p.1,3.
17. John A. Widtsoe, 1965, *op. cit.*, pp. 4-5.
18. Spencer W. Kimball, "Comments to Patriarchs of the Church," October 3,1969. Quoted in The Teachings of Spencer W. Kimball (Bookcraft, 1982), p.506.
19. Joseph F. Smith, *Conference Report,* Oct. 7,1944, p.112.

6

Receiving a Patriarchal Blessing

A Patriarch's Interview and Blessing

Before giving someone a patriarchal blessing, an ordained patriarch will usually hold an informal but personal interview with the person who desires the blessing. In a Church publication we read:

> It is generally considered desirable for a patriarch to sit down and counsel privately with a candidate before giving a blessing. It is well to know something of the candidate's background; his parentage, whether they are members of the Church; his attitudes and aspirations. Information on such matters may serve as a guide respecting the kind of blessing the patriarch might give. By friendly interviewing and wise counseling, mutual understanding and confidence will surely be established. This should be of value both to the patriarch and the one whom he is to bless.[1]

Similarly, another Church publication states:

> Before giving a blessing it is proper and desirable for the patriarch to talk briefly with the one who is to receive the blessing, to get acquainted with him and feel his spirit, and to review the nature and purpose of patriarchal blessings. However, the patriarch should not interview the person for worthiness; this is the responsibility of the bishop or branch president who issues the patriarchal blessing recommend. . . . The blessing should not be given from what the patriarch may know about the person, but rather from the whisperings [and impressions] of the Holy Ghost.[2]

Also, because the nature of patriarchal blessings is "sacred and personal," the Church has strongly recommended that such blessings be given in "private" circumstances:

> Since a patriarchal blessing is a very personal matter, it would appear wise to keep it that way.[3]
> The patriarchal blessing is sacred, confidential, and personal. Therefore, it will be given in private. Family members (parents, husband or wife) may be present.[4]

Following a personal interview with the candidate, the patriarch gives the candidate his or her patriarchal blessing by "laying his hands on the head of the recipient, calling him or her by name," and then pronouncing through divine authority and inspiration an appropriate patriarchal blessing.[5] (To review the "contents of patriarchal blessings" see Chapter 4 of this book.)

Receiving Written Copies
of Patriarchal Blessings

After a person has been given a patriarchal blessing by an ordained patriarch, he or she is entitled to receive a "written" copy of his or her blessing from the patriarch who gave the blessing. This fact has been emphasized by the Church:

> All patriarchal blessings should be recorded [by the patriarch] so that accurate typed copies can be made of each blessing. The blessing may be recorded by a stenographer or on a recording machine. . . . If a malfunction of the machine should occur, the patriarch, as soon as possible, should restore the blessing through prayer and inspiration, giving the blessing a second time if needful. . . . A copy [of the blessing] should be given to [the recipient] as soon as possible. Generally this should be within a week or ten days, never more than two or three weeks. No charge is to be made, nor gratuity accepted, for the blessing. Voice recordings of the blessing for the recipient are not authorized.[6]

In addition, Elder Hyrum G. Smith has stated:

> . . . [Patriarchal] blessings should be written for the purpose of refreshing our memory and aiding us to put them into practice rather than going back every opportunity or every few months or weeks or so, to get another blessing. I have thought, and have been impressed, that this was one of the great reasons why the Lord required us

to make a record of all of the patriarchal blessings that are given by his patriarchs in the Church.[7]

It should also be mentioned that when a "written" or typed copy of a patriarchal blessing is prepared for a recipient, a patriarch also prepares a "duplicate copy" which he places in an official patriarchal "blessing binder" or "record binder" (which belongs to the Church) and which he sends to the Church Historical Department in Salt Lake City when the binder is filled. The Historical Department "indexes, files and microfilms" all patriarchal blessings "for the permanent archives of the Church." If someone should "lose or misplace" their patriarchal blessing a "second copy" of the blessing can be obtained from the Church Historical Department.[8]

Because of the sacred and personal nature of patriarchal blessings, the Church Historical Department has established rules in regard to who can receive copies of patriarchal blessings:

1. A person may obtain a copy of his or her own patriarchal blessing.

2. Husbands and wives may obtain copies of each other's blessings.

3. Parents can obtain copies of their children's blessing.

4. Direct descendants may obtain copies of blessings of their deceased ancestors.

5. Copies of blessings of persons who are under the penalty of excommunication are not given to anyone, unless approved by Church authorities.

(For any additions, exceptions or revisions to these rules contact the Church Historical Department.)[9]

This obvious respect for the sacred and confidential nature of patriarchal blessings has been shown and expressed on many occasions by various General Authorities, one of whom has said:

> A person having received a patriarchal blessing him-self . . . is the one who should have the copy. . . . No one else has a right to a copy of the blessing without his permission, because it is his and belongs to no one else.[10]

One Patriarchal Blessing Is Usually Enough

During the past several decades, the Church has emphasized that "generally one [patriarchal] blessing should be adequate for each person"[11] and that "a second patriarchal blessing generally is not encouraged."[12] Why it is recommended that only one patriarchal blessing be given to an individual by an ordained patriarch is explained by Elder Eldred G. Smith:

> When an ordained patriarch has given a blessing with all the requirements of the declaration of lineage and the sealing blessings and it is on record—recorded in the Church archives—then it is superfluous to keep repeating the same thing over again and putting it on record. It just fills up space in the Historian's Office unnecessarily. The Lord only requires that it be recorded once. Additional blessings may be given, but not necessarily

by a patriarch. These additional blessings should be given by the father who is the patriarch of his home.[13]

People want all of their problems solved in a patriarchal blessing. If it isn't in the patriarchal blessing, they want to come back and get an additional blessing, an accompanying blessing. [Here is an example of] one of the extremes I have actually had: A young man came to me to get a special blessing. When I boiled it down a little bit as to why he wanted another blessing, I found out he and his wife were bickering against each other as to what car they should buy. He wanted to buy the large station wagon. She said, "No, it is too high priced. We can't afford it. We need something cheaper." So he came to me to get a patriarchal blessing, or a special blessing, to help him decide whether he should follow his wife's recommendation. I didn't give him a blessing, but I just took a pencil and paper and figured out for him as he should have done at home with his wife what . . . his income [was]. How much [could he afford for a car? How long [would] it take [him] to pay for it? [Could he] afford that much? Would it be depriving his family of something else to put that much money into a car? Well, that solved the problem for him and so I didn't give him a blessing.[14]

And Elder Hyrum G. Smith has cautioned Latter-day Saints against the extreme of receiving "a multitude of written blessings":

There is always danger in extremes. . . . There are many in the Church who never get a written blessing for their guide or comfort. This is an extreme. It is the privilege and right of every faithful member of the Church to receive a written blessing, for his guide and his comfort, at the hands of certain officers in the Church, and there is little or no excuse for anyone going without this privilege. On the other hand there are others who get a multitude of written blessings, and I have discovered that some have even lost regard for, or faith in, their blessings, because they have received . . . a multitude of many [blessings], and they have discovered a conflict. Therefore, their faith is lost, or they are discouraged, and they lose regard for their blessings. Therefore I say again, beware of extremes.[15]

Notes to Chapter 6

1. R. Clayton Brough, *Statements from Church Publications about Patriarchal Blessings* (West Valley City, Utah: 1983), p .2.
2. *Ibid.,* p.1.
3. *Ibid.,* p.2.
4. *Ibid.,* p.1.
5. See Chapter 5 of this book.
6. R. Clayton Brough, 1983, *op. cit.,* p. 1.
7. Hyrum G. Smith, *Conference Report,* April 6, 1921, pp. 184-185.
8. R. Clayton Brough, 1983, *op. cit.,* p. 1.
9. Conversation between the authors and officials of the Church Historical Department, November 8,1983.
10. Eldred G. Smith, *Conference Report,* April 4,1952, p. 43.
11. R. Clayton Brough, 1983, *op. cit.,* p. 2.
12. *Ibid.,* p.1.

13. Eldred G. Smith, "What Is a Patriarchal Blessing?" (*The Instructor*, February, 1962), p.43.
14. Eldred G. Smith, "Lectures in Theology: Last Message Series" (Salt Lake Institute of Religion, April 30,1971), pp. 5-6.
15. Hyrum G. Smith, 1921, *op. cit.*, p. 184.

7

Understanding a Patriarchal Blessing

How to Understand or Interpret Patriarchal Blessings

Throughout the history of the Church, Patriarchs to the Church, as well as other General Authorities, have offered advice and counsel on how patriarchal blessings can be better understood or interpreted by Latter-day Saints. These remarks by General Authorities can be summarized in the following six statements: (1) in patriarchal blessings people can be from different lineages—even within families; (2) patriarchal blessings do not outline everything that will happen; (3) promises within a patriarchal blessing are conditioned upon faithful living; (4) patriarchal blessings should be viewed from an eternal perspective; (5) people should use discretion when sharing or discussing patriarchal blessings; and (6) patriarchal blessings should be read often, and prayerfully.

To support these statements, each one is treated as a heading followed by remarks various General Authorities have made:

People Can Be from Different Lineages —Even Within Families
(See also Chapter 3)

President Joseph Fielding Smith:

> In giving blessings, the patriarch . . . is directing the lineage through the blood that predominates, and there could be one son who would be designated as of Ephraim and his brother, of the same father and mother, could correctly be said to be of the blood of Manasseh, or of Benjamin, or of any other member of the tribes of Israel.[1]

Eider Eldred G. Smith:

> . . . A person . . . came to me for her Patriarchal Blessing who told me that her father was of Arabian and German extraction. Her mother was Mexican, French and Spanish. In this case I told the individual . . . that if her father came for a blessing he could be pronounced of Judah; her mother, if she came for a blessing, could be pronounced of Manasseh; yet I pronounced their daughter of Ephraim, and people say: "Well, how is that possible?" You see, you're thinking about genealogy. In the father's line there is a mixture of Judah and Ephraim. So the father could be pronounced either of Judah or Ephraim. The mother could be pronounced either of Manasseh or Ephraim. Ephraim was common on both parents,

so I pronounced the daughter to be of Ephraim. Any of the other children could have been pronounced of any of the three tribes.

Now that wasn't so difficult, but this other one is a little bit different. The father was of Portuguese, Spanish, Indian and Hawaiian mixture; his wife was Hawaiian and Chinese. Their daughter married a husband who was Scotch and Portuguese mixture. Then what would the children be? You get all kinds of combinations and mixtures. We are all mixtures. There is no such thing, so far as I have been able to determine, as any one of us being just one lineage and no other mixture in our genealogy at all. As far as genealogy is concerned, or as far as blood line is concerned. So it is the right of the Patriarch to declare which line through which the blessings will come. In other words, he's giving blessings; he's not declaring lineage by terms of just genealogy. He's declaring lineage in terms of blessing. You go to a Patriarch to get a blessing. If you can get that distinction it will help you to understand.[2]

Most people who are pronounced of Ephraim, I think, have literally the blood of Israel, but they may have other mixtures with it so the Patriarch has the right to declare which of these mixtures is going to be the dominant lines in this case. That isn't determined by blood nor by genealogy; it is determined by the inspiration to the Patriarch to declare it such. There are some, now, for instance, [such as] the Orientals. Their national history takes them back previous to the time of Abraham, but they are descendants of "Heber" so they are Hebrews. I understand the term Hebrew and Jew are mixed and used synonymously, but they are not the same. Jews are Hebrews, but not all Hebrews are Jews. Abraham was given the promise that all the nations of the earth should be blessed through his seed. So all the nations of the earth are blessed by being entitled to the blessings of Israel, who are Abraham's descendants. I think there have been mixtures of people who have the blood of Israel mixed in with the Orientals and so they may have a mixture there, too. But they are entitled to the blessings of Israel and they may come in by adoption . . . I do not like the term "adoption"; I never use it in a blessing . . . they may receive the blessings of Ephraim or the blessings of Manasseh by virtue of their faithfulness, which means they are entitled to these blessings because they have become members of the Church and are faithful and receive the blessings through those who are of Israel.[3]

[On August 17, 1977, R. Clayton Brough, one of the authors of this book, had a telephone conversation with Church Patriarch Eldred G. Smith during which Elder Smith mentioned that the number of patriarchal blessings which identified members of the Church as being from some lineage (of the Twelve Tribes of Israel) other than Ephraim, Manasseh or Judah were "very few in number".][4]

From a Church publication:

Many members of the Church are of the lineage of Ephraim, but some are of another lineage—Manasseh, Judah, or one of the other tribes of Israel. Occasionally, when giving a blessing . . . a patriarch may not be inspired to declare a lineage from a specific tribe, but to declare that the individual will receive his blessings through Israel. . . . Occasionally members of the same family receive patriarchal blessings declaring them to be of different lineage. Families are sometimes of mixed lineage, and one lineage will be dominant in one child with a different lineage dominant in another child.[5]

Patriarchal Blessings Do Not Outline Everything That Will Happen

Elder Eldred G. Smith:

Many things are not mentioned in our blessings which come about normally and naturally by our everyday activities and faithfulness. The blessings given by a patriarch are usually the outstanding things which might happen if we work a little harder to get them and exercise a little extra faith. If it were a declaration of all that will happen in our lives, it would take a volume to put it in.[6]

A patriarchal blessing is not a declaration of everything that is supposed to happen in our life. People get the idea that a patriarchal blessing is supposed to tell them everything that is supposed to happen . . . if this were going to be the case it would be what we call fortunetelling. Fortunetelling and patriarchal blessings are as different as black and white. They are entirely opposite from each other. Everything that is going to happen in your life is not supposed to be outlined in your patriarchal blessing.

I have even had missionaries in the field write me a letter and say they have been reading other missionaries' blessings. I don't approve of that in the first place. Then they will mention that other missionaries have been promised blessings regarding marriage, and they ask the question: "My blessing doesn't say anything about marrying. Does that mean I am not supposed to get married?" A priesthood holder, a man holding the Melchizedek Priesthood, imagines that he is not supposed to get married! This is one of his primary priesthood responsibilities. It doesn't have to be in the patriarchal blessing.[7]

Elder John A. Widtsoe:

Necessarily, since patriarchs are but men, they are subject to human frailties. Their manner of speech and thinking is reflected in their blessings. Different men express the same idea in different words. The Lord does not dictate blessings to them word for word. Likewise, portions of the blessing may be emphasized by the nature or desire of the patriarch. Nevertheless, if the patriarch lives worthily, he is sustained by the power and authority of his calling, and will pronounce blessings intended for us. And we, if we live worthily, will comprehend the blessings and find deep comfort in them.[8]

From a Church Publication:

Although a patriarchal blessing is a sacred guideline of information, promises, and counsel from the Lord to help an individual through life, the person receiving a blessing should not expect it to outline all that will happen to him or answer all questions.

If a possible future development, for example marriage or a mission, is not stated in a patriarchal blessing, this does not necessarily mean that it will not come. The Lord, for his purposes, may say certain things to one person in his or her patriarchal blessing and different things to another person.[9]

Promises Within a Patriarchal Blessing Are Conditioned Upon Faithful Living

Elder Hyrum G. Smith:

I trust, my brethren and sisters, that we shall all receive our blessings, and that we shall understand that they are predicated upon obedience to the law of the Lord. The Lord has made the laws upon which our blessings are predicated, and if we observe those laws then the Lord is bound, he says, and we shall receive the blessing; but if we have committed sins which are displeasing before the Lord, if we have broken his commandments, we may deceive his servants here upon the earth, we may deceive the bishops, the presidents, the patriarchs, or other servants of God, perhaps may secure the words of a blessing, but the Lord who gave the commandment, who knows the law, who knows our sins, will not give the blessing until we have rendered obedience unto the law upon which it is predicated. So that. though it may be possible for us to deceive our fellowmen, let us not think that we can deceive the Lord, for he knows our hearts, our desires, our deeds, and will reward us day and night, year in and year out, according to our faithfulness in observing his commandments as they have been given unto us.

So let us, brethren and sisters, learn the laws upon which our blessings are predicated, and then render obedience unto them. Then our promises will be sure and we will not have to practice deception in any way to get a blessing which might otherwise be withheld from us.[10]

Elder Eldred G. Smith:

Many have expressed the thought that if they receive a written patriarchal blessing it will be fulfilled to the letter without any effort on their part.

Which reminds me of the young woman who declared that she was going to be married in the temple when she got married and that was very certain and all her friends understood her attitude, yet when she was married, she not only married out of the temple, but she married a nonmember of the Church. When one of her friends said to her afterwards: "Why, Mary, I thought you, of all people, were going to marry in the temple," she answered, "Well, my patriarchal blessing promised me that I would be married in the temple, so I guess I will some day."

We must serve the Lord diligently and intelligently, keeping all his commandments, if we expect to receive his blessings.

[Then] the question arises[:] if the blessings come from our efforts in righteousness in fulfilling the law upon which the blessing is predicated, why have patriarchal blessings? We will get our blessings anyway, if we live for them. And that is very true, because "we must live for our blessings if we get them, but there comes great comfort and consolation from having our blessings both promised and sealed upon us by authorized servants of the Lord in obedience to his word and law, for the Lord has placed authorized agents on the earth to bear his power and his authority, not only to pronounce, but to seal these blessings, that the Lord may have an anchor upon the souls of men and women forever, for neither death nor the destroyer will end these blessings, but the receiver will possess and enjoy them forever and ever."

A patriarchal blessing gives us courage to live as we know we should live. It helps to keep us from yielding to temptation, to do the things we have been taught to do.[11]

From a Church publication:

All promises and blessings spoken in a patriarchal blessing are conditioned upon the worthy, faithful living of a person receiving the blessing.[12]

Patriarchal Blessings Should Be Viewed from an Eternal Perspective

Elder John A. Widtsoe:

It should always be kept in mind that the realization of the promises made may come in [this] or the future life. Men have stumbled at times because promised blessings have not occurred in this life. They have failed to remember that, in the gospel, life with all its activities continues forever and that the labors of earth may be continued in heaven. Besides, the Giver of the blessings, the Lord, reserves the right to have them become active in our lives, as suits His divine purpose. We and our blessings are in the hands of the Lord. But, there is the general testimony that when the gospel law has been obeyed, the promised blessings have been realized.[13]

Elder Eldred G. Smith:

When I talk about blessings being eternal and what can be accomplished I think of the time element involved . . . not just between birth and until they are thirty or forty or fifty . . . or not from birth until death . . . I think of mortality and the time we have of accomplishing the purposes and developments that mortality gives us; the time between birth and the resurrection. Now, some people say, "So and so was given such and such in his blessing and he died before it was ever fulfilled." Well, so what? That isn't the end of his life or the end of what can be accomplished as the result of mortality. The purpose of mortality or what we can accomplish here is between birth and the resurrection. So many things which we should accomplish in this life and don't get the opportunity to accomplish may be accomplished after death, but before the resurrection. The Lord has said in reference to receiving the Gospel that those who do not receive it in this life, but would have done had they had the opportunity, will receive the blessings of the Celestial Glory. Those are not the exact words, but you will find that in the . . . Doctrine and Covenants [137:7]. By the same token, all these other principles are involved in that same doctrine.

If we keep our own blessing with us and there seem to be things we do not understand, through continued faith, the time will come when the interpretation will be given to us. Some of the interpretations may be fulfilled by our descendants. We are now in a large part fulfilling some of the outstanding blessings given to the children of Israel

by their father. We may not realize all of the blessings in our lifetime. They may be fulfilled after our
death or by our descendants. There is no particular time limit to the fulfillment of blessings. They
are sometimes realized in different ways from
what we expect. But as long as we live worthy of
our blessings, we have an anchor upon the
promise of the Lord that they will be fulfilled.

The fulfillment of all blessings is based on our
faithfulness. We must earn what we get, but we
get what we earn.[14]

Elder LeGrand Richards:

A few years ago . . . my wife and I laid away in
the grave our oldest son, who was nearly sixteen
years of age. . . . Less than a year prior to that we
took him and his younger brother, only sixteen
months difference in their ages, into the office of
the Patriarch of this Church, Brother Hyrum G.
Smith, and he gave them each a blessing.

Now, I ask you, suppose the Patriarch had
known that one of these boys was to die within a
year, could he not promise him anything? What
would it have meant to the eldest son, had he
walked out of the Patriarch's office with no
promise and no blessing, and the younger son
had all the promises and the blessings, for the
older boy truly loved God and kept his commandments.

When that boy passed away, and I met with my
counselors—for I was then President of the Holly-
wood Stake—I said to them: "There is just one
thing, if God could only give us to understand that
boy's blessing." I said: "I wish you brethren would

help us, if you can, so that Sister Richards and I might be comforted."

A few nights after that I took Sister Richards for a ride. We asked the younger boy if he would like to go with us. He said: "No. I think I will stay home." The next morning was Sunday morning. He came in and crawled up on his mother's bed, holding in his hand the two patriarchal blessings, and he said: "Mother, while you were out riding last night I read these blessings." He said: "You see, you haven't understood them."

I think just for the matter of getting it clearly before you I shall read a few words from the two blessings, as they were given by the Patriarch. In the oldest boy's blessing, the one who passed away, the Patriarch said: "For it will be thy privilege to bear the holy Priesthood and to go even among strangers and in strange lands, in defense of truth and righteousness."

This we could not understand. And to the younger boy he said: "For thou shalt bear the holy Priesthood in defense of righteousness and truth, both at home and abroad."

The boy said: "You see, Mother, I am going to labor at home and abroad, but," he said, "LeGrand was to go to strange lands and strange people;" and he said, "They are not on this earth. We know all the lands of this earth and we know all the people that are here."

And to the oldest boy the Patriarch said: "And in due time thy home shall be a fit abode for the spirits of thy loved ones;" and to the younger boy he said: "Thou shalt enjoy the comforts of a happy home and the blessings of honored fatherhood, for thou shalt see thy posterity grow up around thee, to honor thee in the same kind of way in which thou hast honored thy parents." Now, reverse the blessings and give the younger boy's blessing to the older boy, and there would be no explanation. He said: "Mother, you see, LeGrand's home is to be the home of the spirits of his loved ones, and my home is to be here on this earth, where I will see my children grow up around me."

You cannot tell me that God, the Eternal Father, did not give that fourteen-year-old boy the inspiration and revelation to understand these blessings, and our hearts have been comforted.[15]

President Harold B. Lee:

. . . [A] patriarch of [a] stake spoke at [a] funeral . . . [and] said: "When a patriarch pronounces an inspired blessing, such a blessing encompasses the whole of life, not just this phase we call mortality."

"If in this life only we have hope in Christ, we are of all men most miserable," said the Apostle Paul. If we fail to understand this great truth, we will be miserable in time of need, and then sometimes our faith may be challenged. But if we have a faith that looks beyond the grave and trusts in divine Providence to bring all things in their proper perspective in due time, then we have hope, and our fears are calmed. . . . Life does not end with mortal death.[16]

President Joseph Fielding Smith:

Let us say a few words on these patriarchal blessings. Sometimes the individual receiving the blessings can't understand all that's in it. Maybe it's well that he can't, but in course of time the

Lord unfolds to his mind when that blessing becomes fulfilled. There are some things the patriarch may say in a blessing that he has to say rather guardedly, because he couldn't say a direct and simple truth. I call your attention to one: when I was in Canada one time a father came to me with his son's patriarchal blessing. In it the patriarch had said: "In a short time you will be called on an important mission." That's all he said. It was only a few months later when the young man was killed. He was a good, faithful young man. The father said: "That blessing was never fulfilled." I said: "How do you know? Maybe his mission wasn't here."

. . . My uncle, John Smith, who gave as many blessings I suppose as anybody, said one day to me in the presence of others: "When I give a patriarchal blessing, the dividing line between time and eternity disappears." If that be the case, I guess I ought to be willing to accept it. Then there may be things in these blessings that pertain to our future existence. There might be promises made to us that are not fulfilled here that will be fulfilled. For instance, suppose a patriarch says in giving a blessing to a young woman that she shall be married and that she will have posterity, and yet she dies without posterity. Married for time and all eternity in the temple of the Lord, she receives there the blessings of eternal lives, which is a continuation of the seeds forever. Perhaps the patriarch, in giving her a blessing of posterity, sees beyond the veil; so I don't think we should be too hasty in condemning a patriarch when he promises posterity, and then in this life that blessing is not fulfilled. We may ourselves be at fault in judging in matters of this kind.[17]

From a Church publication:

A patriarchal blessing should be viewed from an eternal perspective. Sometimes blessings promised may not come in this life, but may be realized in eternity.[18]

People Should Use Discretion When Sharing or Discussing Patriarchal Blessings

Elder John A. Widtsoe:

It may be added that . . . sacred patriarchal blessings are personal in their nature. They should not be talked about or shown about. . . .[19]

Elder Eldred G. Smith:

I don't recommend . . . reading each other's blessings like missionaries do in reading their companion's blessings and students in school reading their roommate's blessings. This I don't recommend because those outside of your own family don't have the right of interpreting your blessing. Others could very easily misinterpret and misguide. In the interpretation of your blessing, if there is anything that you don't understand, you and your family should find the answer [through such means as faithfulness, effort and prayer]. The Lord will give you the answer at the right time. . . .

Keep the patriarchal blessing within the family. It takes the united efforts of the family to help each other fulfill the blessing. Work together as a family group, and so it is all right for other members of your family to have a copy [of your blessing] if you want them to. No one has a right to a copy of your blessing, or to read it, without your permission. I would recommend you let only those read it, who in your judgement, as a result of their reading it, could help you fulfill it, not just interpret it for you. The interpretation will come to you or members of your family when it will be for the best advantage to you. It will not normally come from strangers or those outside the family.[20]

From Church publications:

Should there be any questions relative to a blessing previously received, these questions should be discussed by the person with the patriarch who gave the blessing if he is available.[21]

A patriarchal blessing is sacred and personal. It should not be read by casual friends or acquaintances. A person may, however, share it with family members.[22]

Patriarchal Blessings Should Be Read Periodically and Prayerfully
(See also Chapter 8)

President Joseph Fielding Smith:

I think you will find that [a patriarchal] blessing, when you receive it, [will] be a great comfort, a guide, and a protection to you. I know blessings are given primarily as guides and protection. We should read them often to keep us from getting into byways and into forbidden paths.[23]

From a Church publication:

A patriarchal blessing should be read periodically and prayerfully.[24]

Notes to Chapter 7

1. Thomas W. Grassley, *Answers to Questions About Patriarchal Blessings* (Springville: 1979), pp. 8-9.
2. Eldred G. Smith, "Patriarchal Blessings," Salt Lake Institute of Religion, January 17,1964, p.3.
3. *Ibid.*, p. 7-8.
4. R. Clayton Brough, *The Lost Tribes* (Bountiful: Horizon Publishers,1979), pp.90-91.
5. R. Clayton Brough, *Statements from Church Publications about Patriarchal Blessings* (West Valley City, Utah: 1983), p.1.
6. Eldred G. Smith, "What Is a Patriarchal Blessing?" (*The Instructor*, February,1962), p. 43.
7. Eldred G. Smith, "Lectures in Theology: Last Message Series" (Salt Lake Institute of Religion, April 30, 1971), p. 5.
8. John A. Widtsoe, "What Is the Meaning of Patriarchal Blessings?" Address to stake presidencies of BYU stakes, 1965, pp. 5-6. (See also *Improvement Era*, January,1942.)
9. R. Clayton Brough,1983, *op. cit.*, p.1.
10. Hyrum G. Smith, *Conference Report*, October 5, 1918, p. 72.
11. Eldred G. Smith, *Conference Report*, April 4, 1973, pp. 29-30.
12. R. Clayton Brough,1983, *op. cit.*, p.1.
13. John A. Widtsoe,1965, *op. cit.*, p. 4.

14. Eldred G . Smith,1964, *op. cit.*, pp.4-5; 1962, *op. cit.*, p.43.
15. LeGrand Richards, *Conference Report*, October 6, 1939, pp. 25-26. (Also quoted in *Follow the Brethren*, Course 17, Teacher's Manual, The Church of Jesus Christ of Latter-day Saints,1975, pp. 38-45.)
16. Harold B. Lee, *From the Valley of Despair to the Mountain Peaks of Hope* (Deseret News Press,1971), pp.8-9.
17. Joseph Fielding Smith, "Address of Joseph Fielding Smith" (BYU Church History and Philosophy 245), June 15, 1956, pp. 5-6.
18. R. Clayton Brough,1983, *op. cit.*, p.1.
19. John A. Widtsoe,1965, *op. cit.*, p. 5.
20. Eldred G. Smith,1971, *op. cit.*, pp. 7-8.
21. R. Clayton Brough,1983, *op. cit.*, p. 3.
22. *Ibid.*, p.1.
23. Joseph Fielding Smith, 1956, *op. cit.*, p. 8.
24. R. Clayton Brough,1983, *op. cit.*, p.1.

8

Living a Patriarchal Blessing

Acquire Appreciation for the Significance of Patriarchal Blessings

In order to really understand and appreciate the significance of a patriarchal blessing, a recipient should "read frequently and ponder" and pray about his or her blessing, and live worthy to receive the blessings and promises mentioned in their patriarchal blessing. This has been stated by several General Authorities, three of whom are quoted below:

Elder John A. Widtsoe has said:

The patriarchal blessing should be read and reread. . . . It . . . should be read frequently and pondered upon for our personal good. . . . It should be made useful in life. This should be done with faith in spiritual blessings. It is a gift of the Lord. The purpose of asking for the blessing must be remembered. It must be read with intelligent consideration of its meaning. Attention should be fixed upon the one great meaning of the blessing rather than upon particular statements. There must be no quibbling about the time or place when the promises should be fulfilled or about the man who gave it. As the blessing was given through the inspiration of the Lord, so its meaning will be made clear by the same power; and its fulfillment will be in His hands.[1]

Elder Eldred G. Smith has stated:

Sit down and read your patriarchal blessing . . . at times when you are disturbed, distressed, discouraged and not satisfied with your life. To read your patriarchal blessing sometimes gives you courage and brings you back to where you started. It gets you in the right groove again. It gets your mind set on the proper goals. . . . It can give you a little extra courage . . . when you need it the most.[2]

And Elder Hyrum G. Smith has said:

. . . I should like to admonish my brethren and sisters to read their [patriarchal blessings] carefully and not to be easily discouraged and think that because their blessing is short it is incomplete, or because it contains only a few promises, that there is something else that has not been written or has not been promised. Yet, it is true that all the blessings and all the promises that the Lord has in store for us are not embodied in one written blessing; . . . but that written blessing is a guide, and it is a key in a way, through your faithfulness, to the blessings which are promised unto the faithful, and may be an index to your whole life.[3]

Faithfulness Brings Fulfillment
of Patriarchal Blessings

As stated in Chapter 7 of this book, Elder John A. Widtsoe has said that "it should always be kept in mind that realization of the promises made [in a patriarchal blessing] may come in [this] or the future life . . . [and that] there is the general testimony that when the gospel law has been obeyed, the promised blessings have been realized." In addition to this statement, Elder Widtsoe has stated:

> Above all, it must ever be remembered that every blessing is conditioned upon our faithfulness. Let us examine our lives from time to time to learn whether we are so living as to be worthy of the blessings promised. It is certain that our patriarchal blessing, if we give it proper respect, may be a source of divine help in life's journey.[4]

In conclusion, President Spencer W. Kimball has specifically born his testimony to the fact that "none of the blessings [a patriarch] pronounces will fail if the participant of the blessing fully subscribes" to living worthily and fulfilling his or her obligations to the Lord:

> The patriarch is a prophet entitled to the revelations of the Lord to each individual on whose head he places his hands. He may indicate the lineage of the individual, but he may also pour out blessings that are prophetic to the individual for his life. We hope the people of this land will avail themselves of this great blessing. The blessings which he gives are conditional. They are promised,

as are most other blessings that the Lord has promised to people, contingent upon their worthiness and fulfilling the obligations. There is no guarantee that the blessings will be fulfilled unless the individual subscribes to the program, but I bear my testimony to you that none of the blessings he pronounces will fail if the participant of the blessing fully subscribes.[5]

Notes to Chapter 8

1. John A. Widtsoe, "What Is the Meaning of Patriarchal Blessings?" Address to stake presidencies of BYU stakes, 1965, p. 5. (See also *Improvement Era*, January, 1942.)
2. Eldred G. Smith, "Lectures in Theology: Last Message Series" (Salt Lake Institute of Religion, April 30, 1971), p. 7.
3. Hyrum G. Smith *Conference Report*, April 6, 1921, p. 185.
4. John A. Widtsoe, "What Is the Meaning of Patriarchal Blessings?" *op. cit.*, p. 5.
5. Spencer W. Kimball, "Priesthood Session, Seoul, Korea Area Conference," August 17, 1975. Quoted in *The Teachings of Spencer W. Kimball* (Bookcraft, 1982), p. 504.

Bibliography

Books

Bible. King James Version.

Book of Mormon.

Brough, Clayton R. *The Lost Tribes: History, Doctrine, Prophecies and Theories About Israel's Lost Ten Tribes.* Bountiful: Horizon Publishers, 1979.

Church Almanac 1981, Deseret News, 1980.

Doctrine and Covenants.

Kimball, Spencer W. *The Teachings of President Spencer W. Kimball,* Salt Lake City: Bookcraft, 1982.

McConkie, Bruce R. *Mormon Doctrine* Salt Lake City: Bookcraft, 1966.

Pearl of Great Price.

Smith, Joseph. *Teachings of the Prophet Joseph Smith.* Salt Lake City: Deseret Book, 1939.

Widtsoe, John A. *Priesthood and Church Government.* Salt Lake City: Deseret Book, 1939.

Young, S. Dilworth. *Family Night Reader, A Young Peoples Guide in Gospel Study.* Salt Lake City: Bookcraft, 1958.

Periodicals

Church Almanac 1981, Deseret News, 1980.

Richards, LeGrand. "A Chosen Vessel Unto Me." *The Instructor,* Dec. 1964.

Smith, Eldred G. "What Is a Patriarchal Blessing?" *The Instructor,* Feb.1962.

Smith, Hyrum G. "Patriarchs and Patriarchal Blessings." *Improvement Era,* May 1930.

Taylor, John. "Patriarchal." *Times and Seasons,* June 1, 1845. Number 6.

Widtsoe, John A. "What Is the Meaning of Patriarchal Blessings?" *Improvement Era,* January, 1942.

Miscellaneous

Brough, R. Clayton. "Statements from Church Publications about Patriarchal Blessings." West Valley City, 1983.

Grassley, Thomas W. "Answers to Questions About Patriarchal Blessings." Springville, 1979.

Grassley, Thomas W., "Survey on Patriarchal Blessings," Provo, Utah, 1976.

Kemp, Thomas Jay, "The Office of Patriarch to the Church," Stanford, Connecticut, 1972.

Kimball, Spencer W. *Conference Report,* October, 1977.

———. "The Ordinances of the Gospel." Provo: Address to Seminary and Institute Teachers at Brigham Young University, 1962.

Lee, Harold B. "From the Valley of Despair to the Mountain Peaks of Hope." Salt Lake City: Deseret News Press, 1971.

McOmber, Calvin Jr. "The Historical Development of the Patriarchal Priesthood," History of Religion 645, BYU, July 18, 1962.

Richards, LeGrand. *Conference Report.* October, 1939.

———. "Patriarchal Blessings." Provo: Address to BYU Studentbody, May 27, 1953.

Smith, Eldred G. *Conference Report.* April, 1952.

——. *Conference Report.* April, 1971.

——. *Conference Report.* April, 1973.

——. "Lectures in Theology: Last Message Series." Address to Salt Lake Institute of Religion, April, 30, 1971.

——. "Patriarchal Blessings." Salt Lake Institute of Religion, January 17, 1964.

Smith, Hyrum, G. *Conference Report.* October, 1918.

——. *Conference Report.* April, 1921.

——. *Conference Report.* April, 1924.

Smith, Joseph F. *Conference Report.* October 7, 1944.

Smith, Joseph Fielding. "Address of President Joseph Fielding Smith," Church History and Philosophy 245, BYU, June 15, 1956.

Widtsoe, John A. "What Is the Meaning of Patriarchal Blessings?" Stake Presidencies of BYU Stakes, 1965.

Index

A

Abraham, 11
Adam, 11
Age to receive patriarchal blessings, 63

B

Brough, R. Clayton, 84

C

Clark, J. Reuben, Jr., 31
Comfort and encouragement, 48
Copies, receiving, 75

D

Declaration of lineage, 43, 55
Definition of a patriarchal blessing, 11, 31
Different Lineages—even within families, 82

E

Encouragement and comfort, 48
Enos, 11
Evangelist, 12

F

Father's blessings, 25, 26, 32, 33, 34, 35, 36, 37
First patriarchal blessings, 13

G

Gifts, spiritual, 56

H

Hinckley, Alonzo A., 39, 40
History of patriarchal blessings, 11

I

Inheritances to ancient Israel, 56
Interpreting patriarchal blessings, 81

J

Jacob, 11

K

Kimball, Spencer W., 22, 34, 56, 62, 69

L

Lee, Harold B., 23, 63, 93
Lineage, declaration of, 43, 55
Lineages, different—even within families, 82
Literal blood lineage, 56
Living a patriarchal blessing, 99

M

McKay, David O., 31

N

Natural patriarchs, 24, 25, 26

O

Ordained patriarchs, 24

P

Patriarchal Age, 11
Patriarchal blessing(s),
    as a guidepost, 47, 61
    as personal scripture, 49

compared to fortune-telling, 37, 38, 39
definition of, 11, 31
for children that are mentally or physically
    handicapped, 62
fulfillment of according to our faithfulness, 24,
    31, 39, 43, 53, 55-57, 87, 91, 95, 100, 101
in Christ's time, 12
preparing for, 61
purpose of, 16, 43
steps in obtaining, 67
structure of, 53-55, 57
Patriarch(s),
    as a prophet, seer and revelator, 19
    as an office in the Melchizedek Priesthood,
      11, 18
    how they are chosen, 17
    preparation of, 21
    succession of, 14, 16
Predestination, 38
Prophetic statement of the life mission, 55

R

Richards, George F., 15
Richards, LeGrand, 12, 26, 46, 91
Richards, Stephen L., 31

S

Scriptural examples of patriarchal blessings, 58
Sealing blessings, 46
Seth, 11
Smith, Asael, 15
Smith, Eldred G., 14, 25, 35, 37, 44, 48, 56, 57,
    63, 66, 77, 82, 84, 85, 88, 90, 95, 100
Smith, Hyrum G., 15, 47, 48, 55, 65, 75, 78, 87,
    91, 100
Smith, Hyrum, 15

Smith, John, 15
Smith, Joseph, 12, 13
Smith, Joseph F., 14, 16, 33, 69
Smith, Joseph Fielding, 23, 24, 33, 39, 62, 63, 82, 93, 96
Smith, Joseph Sr., 13, 14, 15, 47
Smith, Nicholas, 15
Smith, William, 14

T

Taylor, John, 16

U

Understanding a patriarchal blessing, 81

W

When to receive a patriarchal blessing, 63
Widtsoe, John A., 16, 31, 32, 39, 43, 49, 58, 62, 68, 86, 89, 95, 99
Written Copies, receiving, 75

Y

Young, S. Dilworth, 56

About the Authors

Robert Clayton Brough holds a Master of Science degree in Geography from Brigham Young University. He is a television weather forecaster for KTVX-TV in Salt Lake City, is president Of Atmospheric Consultants, and teaches science at Springville Junior High School.

During the past ten years, Elder Brough has lectured extensively and written several books and professional papers on geography, history, climatology and agriculture. He is also the author of four books dealing with LDS theology: *His Servants Speak, They Who Tarry, Our First Estate* and *The Lost Tribes*. His church experience includes completion of a full-time mission to the Eastern states, labors as a stake missionary, scoutmaster, genealogist, gospel doctrine teacher, counselor in a bishopric, high priest instructor, assistant stake clerk, and assistant stake executive secretary.

Elder Brough is the son of Marshall and Utahna Brough of Orem, Utah. In 1973 he married Ethel Mickelson, daughter of Clark and Helen Mickelson of Grace, Idaho. The Brough's have four children and reside in Wet Valley City, Utah.

Thomas William Grassley holds a Master of Arts degree in Organizational Communications from Brigham Young University. He is the owner of Carnival Concessions, Carnival Movie Rental, and Minute Man Pizza in Springville, and The Sticker Shop in the University Mall, Orem, Utah.

Elder Grassley's church experience includes completion of a full-time mission to the Northern states, counselor in an elders quorum presidency, Sunday School teacher and activities chairman.

He is the son of Carl and Alice Grassley of Santa Clara, Utah. In 1978 he married Susan Towse, daughter of Kenneth and Margaret Towse of Los Angeles, California. The Grassley's have two children and reside in Springville, Utah.